Contents

To find an establishment, look for it's entry number on each p

GW00373287

vouchers

All the usuals plus our **Special FOODIE Vouchers** for this year, find them at the back

award

Nominate your favourite restaurant for an award and you could win a meal for two

Key to symbols

Families welcome	Extensive wines by the glass (10 or more)	Smoking area provided	FOODIE reader recommended
Wheel chair access	Real ale	Chef profile	£5 off VOUCHER
Garden/patio area	Live music or entertainment	FT Fair Trade produce used where possible	10% off VOUCHER
Accommodation available	Conference room	O Organic produce used where possible	Free bottle of **wine** VOUCHER
Extensive Wine List (30 or more)	Dog friendly	DC Dining Card	V Special FOODIE VOUCHER

Average cost of 3 course meal without drinks

A	£20 or below	D	£30 - £35
B	£20 - £25	E	£35 - £40
C	£25 - £30	F	£40 or above

THE FOODIE voucher symbols: Please check individual entries for which FOODIE vouchers are accepted and any establishment terms (terms and conditions apply)

Introduction

Our lives are full of choices; luckily some are easy to make with just a little well-informed knowledge. That's where THE FOODIE GUIDE becomes invaluable. For where there is so much choice available when it comes to food, whether eating in or eating out, we notice more and more of you are turning to our pages either for some inspiration when it comes to cooking at home, or where to go when you deserve a night off. And after eleven years of listening to our readers, we think that local is definitely best! Whether you're searching for the perfect coffee bean or the treat of your dreams, we are confident you'll be satisfied by the taste experiences that await you.

There's more to this region than meets the eye, our local chefs are some of the very best you will find anywhere in the world, we know because you've told us about them, that's why we're passing it on. Why not find out for yourself by using THE FOODIE GUIDE to explore locally and if you discover some great places to eat out or to buy your goodies from which we haven't included in this edition, then we will be very pleased to hear from you.

Paul Allen
Editor

Foreword

by our guest chef for this year
Chris Smith

Working in an industry with such long and unsociable hours and working in an environment under such massive pressure will confuse people when I say that I have the best job there is out there. With the ability to create whatever I like on a daily basis keeps me excited and to show who I am in a plate of food gives me so much pleasure but also responsibility, to make sure every plate of food goes out perfectly.

When I was sixteen years old Peter Chandler was teaching me how to make a Dauphinoise Potato and now I find it remarkable to think that ten years on I am still passing on his knowledge to my young and enthusiastic chefs. And I hope this will become a cycle that carries on for years to come. Therefore, it is these chefs that have passed on their skills, which help to create the quality of eateries that we now have in this beautiful part of the country.

We are very lucky to have such a diverse and top quality group of restaurants in our area, we are truly spoilt for choice and with this I'd like to thank everyone involved with The Foodie Guide and its success in bringing all the top restaurants in the area together.

All this said and done, it is ultimately our customers who have helped grow and evolve what we think of food today, because without them we would have no reason to cook, we would have no reason to create and we would have no reason to push the boundaries of cuisine.

Chris Smith
Head Chef
The Three Tuns

Food for thought

My first experience around food came when I was five. I remember - and always will - going over to my granny's bungalow in Totternhoe for Sunday Roast. Help was always needed in the kitchen, especially with the creation of Yorkshire Puddings - flour would always fly around the room if I was involved.

My granny had a real passion for food. She would use meat from her local butchers and make her own jams and marmalade to accompany the raft of desserts and cakes which would be served up after the main meal, whether we were full or not.

The family Sunday Lunch was always something I looked forward to. It was fun and, obviously, delicious. I believe that to create something special in the kitchen you need that enjoyment. If you put all your love into it you will get the rewards back. From that first point of preparing Yorkshires I was in love with food and all it stood for: fun, family and flavour. The thing I found most exciting about cooking wasn't just the food itself, or the consumption of it, it was the experience and how it brought everyone together.

It soon became clear to me that food was a major part of family life. My granny also worked in her local pub's kitchen and my mum used to cook at the village primary school which my brother and I attended in Westoning.

Gradually I was learning what cooking meant and how it was done. I was intrigued at how simple ingredients such as flour, eggs, butter and sugar could be combined to make the most delightful victoria sandwiches. I'd be transfixed beside the oven, watching it rise majestically from the tin.

As I began my own experiments in our (or, my mum's) kitchen, I was learning from a young age that not everything would work how you'd want or expect. Why wasn't the end product like the recipe promised? Eggs might be smaller, flour might be finer, ovens might be hotter. It was frustrating at the time but, as I would go on to find out, experimenting in the kitchen is one of the most rewarding things when you concoct something special - occasionally by accident.

It was when I was in Year 10 at school that I knew which direction I wanted my career to go. When I was asked what kind of work experience I wanted to do during Year 10 work placement, I explained I was interested in becoming a chef. And that's where it all began.

I was a nervous, shy, but excited 15-year-old that was sent to Flitwick Manor, a restaurant a five-minute drive from our home at the time. I remember going into the kitchen and meeting the head chef, Richard Walker, together with his jovial group of chefs. Once I witnessed them at work I knew I hadn't a clue of what they were doing, but it only heightened my interest in becoming one of them. Desperate to learn the art and to be involved, Richard showed me how to chop for the first time. After one day in the kitchen I came home to my parents and told them both I wanted to be a chef. The idea of a practical job, where I'd always continue to learn, really appealed to me.

A year later, once I'd turned 16, I went back to Flitwick Manor as a kitchen porter. Richard said to me once I'd washed enough pots and pans I could help the pastry section. Believe me, those pots and pans where washed in double-quick time. I was desperate to show everyone what I could do. I was in awe of the chefs and after successfully helping with a soufflé or two, I was sent back to the sink. Seeing the mountain of pots and pans waiting for me gave me the determination and drive to succeed as a chef.

Having washed and scrubbed my way around the kitchen I was given the opportunity to become a part-time chef at Flitwick Manor. Still a young boy, and not yet 18, I absolutely loved going into work at the weekends. It gave me a real buzz. Whether it was 50 covers in the evening or breakfast the following morning, I loved every minute of it.

Richard taught me everything, and it was him who told me to go to Barnfield College in Luton to enable me to get the right qualifications. College was okay, but it was the hands-on work in the kitchen with Richard and his team that I craved. The one-on-one education I received was unbelievable and I am ever so grateful for his time and tuition. It was fantastic and a privilege to be able to learn from somebody like Richard.

After three years of full-time work at Flitwick Manor I moved to Rushton Hall in Northamptonshire where I worked under another fine chef, Adrian Coulthard. It was Adrian who taught me the complex style of cooking. His approach to food was to take one ingredient and use it in various different ways, and this was something that I was really impressed with and hadn't learned before.

Two years at Rushton Hall followed before I moved to Devon for three years. Why? The idea was to move to a different area of the country, an area famed for its rural style of cooking and fantastic local produce. That was where my development of a chef sky-rocketed. Over the course of this period, I also had the support of my fiancée Lucy, a hugely talented pastry chef.

I'd been around food all of my young adult life. I was learning new things all the time and in 2011 I decided to apply to go on the BBC's Masterchef: The Professionals television programme. To get through the application process and, ultimately, to the final of the competition, was the greatest achievement of my career to date. My performance was a nod to those who had helped me reach that point: my family, Lucy, and Richard all those years ago when I was a fresh-faced, wide-eyed boy at Flitwick Manor.

Now I'm 27 and have been head chef at St Helena in Elstow, near Bedford, since November 2012. Together with Lucy and my right-hand man Ali Johnson, we have worked tirelessly to produce fresh, tasty, modern food from local ingredients. We respect the food and showcase it in a modern style.

My future goals are, of course, to win awards, with a Michelin star the ultimate ambition. However, it is my love for cooking that I have had since I was a little boy that gives me the drive and determination to be the best chef - and I don't think that will ever change.

One day I'd love to own my own restaurant and be the chef that teaches the next 15 year old who comes in for work experience, just like Richard did with me. There's no better achievement in life than seeing someone who you've nurtured go on and achieve great things.

For more information and to read the St Helena menu visit http://www.sthelenarestaurant.com/

Steve Barringer
Head Chef
St Helena Restaurant

1

London Road
Little Kingshill
Great Missenden
Bucks HP16 0DG
Tel: 01494 862200
Fax: 01494 862945
Email: goodfood@nagsheadbucks.com
www.nagsheadbucks.co.uk

AA Rosette for Culinary Excellence
AA 4 Star Inn, AA Pick of the Pubs
"Food Pub of the Year" – The Publican Regional Award
BBC's Countryfile, "Top 55 UK Pubs to Eat & Stay"

The Nags Head in Great Missenden, Buckinghamshire is a traditional 15th century country Inn and restaurant situated along the valley of the River Misbourne in the glorious Chiltern Hills.

Brought to you by the Michaels family, owners of the award-winning Bricklayers Arms in Flaunden, Hertfordshire, the newly refurbished Nags Head serves an Anglo French fusion menu. The Nags Head has now been awarded with its first "Rosette" for its "Culinary Excellence" and accredited in several guides including a Commendation Award in the Hardens Guide; chosen as "Pick of the Pubs" in the AA Pub Guide and a recommendation and on the front cover of the Michelins "Eating Out in Pubs" and the much coveted "Michelin Guide".

The Nags Head was recently featured in the movie, Mr Fantastic Fox as it was an old favourite of children's author, Roald Dahl. You can also see executive head chef, Claude Paillet cook on Sky TV channel, Planet Food, at the Nags Head, cooking the great Sunday roast. If you miss one of the repeats, you can view it on 'YouTube'.

Dining guests will receive a warm welcome at the newly refurbished Nags Head. It has still kept all of its original features, including a large inglenook fireplace and low old oak beams, and many new features including a new bar and stylish new furnishings throughout.

THE FOODIE GUIDE
Diner Review

"Exciting combinations of flavours and textures, and a very welcoming atmosphere."

Now graded as an AA 4 star Inn, there are half a dozen new double and twin bedrooms, all beautifully refurbished with bath or shower ensuites After a rested night's sleep, you'll find a hearty breakfast waiting for you in the morning.

Food is our passion; we use only the finest produce when available because we know it makes a difference and wherever possible, we source from local farms and suppliers. We believe in giving good value for money and serve only the finest quality food, so you can be assured of an excellent meal, time and time again. On the lunch and evening menus, you'll find favourites, such as home smoked fishes; mixed and wild mushroom feuillette; our famous 21 day aged Bedfordshire Fillet Steaks with a selection of sauces along with a great steak and kidney ale pie and local game. Fresh fish dishes are sourced according to market availability and change on a daily basis.

Don't miss out on our Sunday roasts where you'll find locally supplied fresh produce and mouthwatering puddings, along with an extensive award winning wine list to suit all tastes, as well as a selection of local ales.

Our bar is a great place to relax in front of the open fireplace and in the summer months you can enjoy a drink or meal in our delightful garden with attractive views of rolling hills of the Chilterns.

Food service times:
Mon-Sat 12.00 pm - 2.30 pm & 6.30 - 9.30 pm
Sun 12.00 pm - 3.30 pm & 6.30pm - 8.30 pm

£5

Fremantle Room

Dining Hall

Located in the lovely village of Swanbourne North Buckinghamshire is The Betsey Wynne, which forms part of the Swanbourne estate, which has been in the Fremantle family for over 200 years. Named after one of the Estate's colourful ancestors the opening of The Betsey Wynne is the result of many years of careful planning by the Estate and a quiet determination by the present owner to preserve and promote country life.

Built in a true local style, this free house has a large bar with comfortable leather sofas, open log fires for those truly cold evenings and an impressive oak beamed dining hall. New this year is the "Fremantle Room" and provides the perfect place for private parties, corporate functions and conferences. This room has been designed to be totally self contained with it's own washroom, bar and private patio areas. It is equipped with state of the art audio and visual systems, full conferencing support and bespoke refreshments and menus to suit.

The Betsey Wynne is a true "local" farm pub. Using the farm's own fresh produce and as far as possible supporting local farmers who supply the wonderful restaurant. The beef comes from the Home Farm's herd of pedigree Aberdeen Angus cows. The lamb on the menu comes from the flock of pedigree Hampshire Down sheep, which some butchers refer to as the "Aberdeen Angus equivalent of the lamb counter". They have exceptional eating quality - juicy, tender and a wonderful flavour. The pork comes from a variety of local producers. Sausages are made by Betsy Duncan Smith, who also cures her hams for the pub from her Saddleback and Large Black pigs. Both are traditional native breeds, full of flavour and reared traditionally in Swanbourne. Poultry is sourced from various local suppliers depending on produce required for menus. Seasonal game and venison is sourced where possible from nearby estates and primarily the Claydon Estate. From time to time 'specials' include pheasant, partridge, pigeon and rabbit.

The Estate has reinstated a traditional orchard to produce apples, pears, plums, mulberries, quince and figs. The Fremantle family's walled garden has also been revived and under Philip Dalton, the head gardener, now produces herbs and a variety of vegetables and soft fruit.

Loyalty cards and gift vouchers are also on offer.

THE FOODIE GUIDE
Diner Review

"The quality is outstanding, with an abundance of variety on offer for all tastes."

Food service times:
Mon - Fri 12.00 pm - 2.30 pm & 7.00 pm - 9.30 pm
Sat 12.00 pm - 9.30 pm
Sun 12.00 pm - 4.00 pm (8.00 pm summer) Sunday menu only

Vouchers accepted
Monday to Thursday only

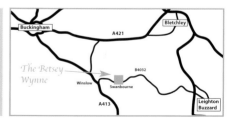

THE BETSEY WYNNE

21 Mursley Road
Swanbourne
Buckinghamshire
MK17 0SH
Tel: 01296 720825
Email: info@thebetseywynne.co.uk
www.thebetseywynne.co.uk

the swan inn

Broughton Road
Milton Keynes Village
Milton Keynes
Buckinghamshire MK10 9AH
Tel: 01908 665240
Fax: 01908 395081
Email: info@theswan-mkvillage.co.uk
www.theswan-mkvillage.co.uk

This 13th Century thatched pub features flagstone floors, an open fire set in an inglenook fireplace and a sheltered orchard garden. Sympathetically renovated, the interior is an eclectic mix of traditional charm and contemporary chic with warm fabrics and clever use of natural finishes. The dining room overlooks a terrace set in the garden and is ideal for summer dining.

Real ales feature alongside an extensive wine list boasting over 20 wines by the glass and the range of soft drinks include a selection of organic fruit juices and lemonades. An open plan kitchen prepares a simple yet creative menu, changed monthly in line with the seasons, based on excellent value and local ingredients, including herbs from its own garden.

Sunday lunch is a traditional affair with a selection of succulent roasts and plentiful veg and potatoes. Daily changing specials plus a selection of lighter lunch items complete the food offer.

Service is brisk and friendly by the knowledgeable staff who herald from around the globe. The atmosphere is always lively given the core group of locals who support this warm and welcoming pub in the heart of the original Milton Keynes Village. A real find.

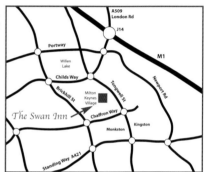

THE FOODIE GUIDE
Diner Review

"The food has exceptional taste and quality. The service is excellent."

Food service times:
Mon-Thur 12.00 pm - 3.00 pm & 6.00 pm - 9.30 pm
Fri-Sat 12.00 pm - 3.00 pm & 6.00 pm - 10.00 pm
Sun 12.00 pm - 6.00 pm

£5 10%

The Carriage House Restaurant

Claydon House, Middle Claydon
Buckinghamshire MK18 2EX
Tel: 01296 730004
Email: eat@thecarriagehouserestaurant.co.uk
www.thecarriagehouserestaurant.co.uk

Adjacent to the magnificent Claydon House, a National Trust property you'll find The Carriage House Restaurant, a hidden gem and a must for foodies who love delicious, honest and well cooked food. A great independent restaurant and venue for private parties and extremely well priced.

Menus change seasonally with Head Chef/Proprietor Tim Matthews offering you beautiful and imaginative modern British cuisine using locally sourced produce and the fabulous fruits and veg from the on-site walled kitchen garden.

Tim trained at Westminster College long before the likes of Jamie Oliver, worked extensively in London and finished his training at the Montreaux Palace, coming to Claydon after running "Rosamund The Fair" Oxford's cruising restaurant with his wife and partner Sophia.

Full restaurant details and Special Events are listed on their website including annual mushroom forays with John Wright from The River Cottage, pre-theatre suppers, garden feasts and Christmas menus. And on Sundays you'll find indulgent 2 or 3-course lunches.

THE FOODIE GUIDE
Diner Review

"Lots of talent here, the food is amazing and the restaurant is in a very special setting too."

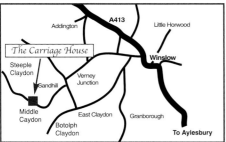

Map showing The Carriage House near Middle Claydon, with A413, Addington, Little Horwood, Winslow, Steeple Claydon, Sandhill, Verney Junction, East Claydon, Granborough, Botolph Claydon, To Aylesbury.

Food service times:
Mon-Wed 12.00 pm - 3.00 pm
Thur-Fri Closed **Sat-Sun** 12.00 pm - 3.00 pm
Saturday evenings from 6.00 pm and Special Event timing from our website (bookings required).
Private parties and weddings at any time throughout the year.

Lunch Dinner

£5

The Crooked Billet

2 Westbrook End
Newton Longville
Buckinghamshire
MK17 0DF
Tel: 01908 373936
Fax: 01908 631979
www.thebillet.co.uk

THE FOODIE GUIDE
Diner Review

"This place is a foodie's delight, with satisfying and surprising food."

A contemporary award winning restaurant in a traditional country pub

"THE FOODIE Award 2004, 2006, 2007, 2010, 2011 & 2012 - Bucks" - THE FOODIE GUIDE
"50 best restaurants in the UK" - The Independent Guide
"Gastro Pub Of The Year" - The Times
"Wine Pub Of The Year" - The Good Pub Guide
"Inspectors Favourite Restaurant" - Michelin Guide to Pubs
"One of the best restaurants outside of London" - Tatler Guide

Milton Keynes Restaurant of the year 2012. The Crooked Billet is a contemporary restaurant located in a traditional, thatched, British pub in the village of Newton Longville, 7 miles from Milton Keynes in Buckinghamshire.

Monthly changing A la Carte menu and daily changing lunch and dinner set menus showcase seasonal, locally sourced ingredients. While the extensive wine list offers some 200 wines by the glass.

You can enjoy simpler dishes, snacks and sandwiches in the bar area which has original oak beams and inglenook fireplaces. The real ale is credited with Cask Marque and Brewers Awards and the cheeseboard is one of the best in the country.

Please visit our website for up-to-date menus and events.

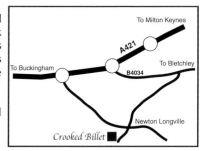

Food service times:
Lunch - **Tues-Sat** 12.00 pm - 2.00 pm **Sun** 12.30 pm - 4.00 pm
Dinner - **Mon-Thurs** 7.00 pm - 9.30 pm **Fri-Sat** 6.30 pm - 10.00 pm

Vouchers not valid Fri or Sat evening

Main Street
Adstock
Buckinghamshire
MK18 2JN
Tel: 01296 712584
Fax: 01296 715375
Email: enquiries@theoldthatchedinn.co.uk
www.theoldthatchedinn.co.uk

The Old Thatched Inn

Gastro Pub, Adstock

THE FOODIE GUIDE
Diner Review

"The service was excellent, the food fresh and tasty, the surroundings relaxed - perfection!"

Aylesbury Vale's Village Pub of the Year 2010, The Old Thatched Inn is a countryside gastro-pub which offers its customers a unique blend of high quality dining hosted in a relaxed and comfortable environment. Situated in the picturesque village of Adstock, Buckinghamshire, The Old Thatched Inn dates back to 1702 and combines this heritage with a menu that fuses the freshest seasonal ingredients cooked with emphasis on taste, with modern presentation.

Managed by owner and ex-chef Andrew Judge and his wife Lisa, the team at the locally-celebrated Old Thatched Inn believes in casual dining and sources the finest, freshest ingredients from a multitude of small specialist food producers and suppliers, preferring local and organic produce whenever possible.

Favourites on the seasonally-changing menu include locally sourced rare-breed lamb, an extensive fish selection delivered direct from Billingsgate market, and home-made ice creams, with further specials that change daily which excite the mind and the palate. The Old Thatched Inn also boasts a wine list featuring close to 40 selections and is one of the only gastro-pubs in the county to have five fine ales on tap along with a vast shelf selection of malt whiskies and other spirits from across the globe.

With five qualified chefs and eight full and part-time waiting staff, the service at The Old Thatched Inn is professional, attentive and discrete. A welcoming and comfortable waiting lounge, a generous bar area seating 35 and large conservatory seating 60 people, make The Old Thatched Inn the ideal venue for both casual dining, business lunches and special events.

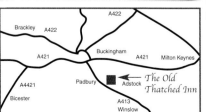

Brackley A422 A422
A421 Buckingham A421 Milton Keynes
A4421 Padbury Adstock *The Old Thatched Inn*
Bicester A413 Winslow

Opening times: 12 noon - 11.00 pm
Food served: **Mon-Fri** 12 noon - 2.30 pm & 6.00 - 9.30 pm
Sat 12 noon - 9.30 pm **Sun** 12 noon - 8.00 pm
Restaurant times may vary due to season

£5 10%
Vouchers valid Mon-Thurs

THE FOODIE AWARD
2013
Buckinghamshire
winner
as voted by
THE FOODIE GUIDE readers

Cameron's Brasserie is located in the historic coaching town of Stony Stratford. We pride ourselves on serving fresh innovative food created by award-winning Chef Owner Dan Cameron. Open for lunch Tuesday to Sunday and dinner Tuesday to Saturday, Cameron's boasts diverse and regularly changing menus including à la carte, Tasting and Fixed Price options.

Despite being just 29 years of age, Dan Cameron has already accumulated a long list of career achievements. Upon completion of his diploma at Leith's School of Food and Wine, Dan went on to work at some of London's most notable restaurants. Cameron's Brasserie opened in July 2011 and has built itself an excellent reputation for food in a relaxed and inviting atmosphere.

Venue hire
Cameron's Brasserie is available for exclusive private hire and is an ideal location for a special birthday, wedding reception, or product launch. For parties up to 18 please call to book or use our online booking system. Parties over 18 requiring a single table or up to 100 for canapés and drinks reception will need to exclusively hire the whole restaurant.

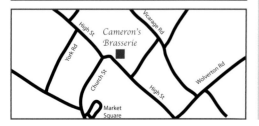

Opening times:
Mon Closed
Tue - Fri 12.00 pm - 3.00 pm & 6.30 pm - 10.00 pm
Sat 9.30 am - 3.00 pm & 6.30 pm - 10.00 pm
Sun 12.00 pm - 5.00 pm

Food service times:
Tue - Sat 12.00 pm - 2.30 pm & 6.30 pm - 9.00 pm
(Food served till 9.30pm Fri & Sat)
Sun 12.00 pm - 4.00 pm

THE FOODIE GUIDE
Diner Review

"Fabulous, inventive dishes, fresh and appealing."

5 Odells Yard
High Street
Stony Stratford
Milton Keynes
Buckinghamshire MK11 1AQ
Tel: 01908 568000
Email: info@camerons-brasserie.co.uk
www.camerons-brasserie.co.uk

Buckinghamshire eating out Buckinghamshire

Rajdhani

706 Midsummer Boulevard
Food Centre
Central Milton Keynes
MK9 3NT
Tel: 01908 392299
Fax: 01908 392541
Email: rajdhanimk@yahoo.co.uk
www.rajdhanimk.com

THE FOODIE GUIDE
Diner Review

"Excellent service here and lovely fresh dishes, with an extensive menu to choose from."

"As featured on BBC's Look East"

The Rajdhani restaurant owned and managed by Ali is regularly rated in the top 100 Indian restaurants and was recently positioned in the top 10 for The Best Spice Restaurant in the UK 2012 and was awarded silver for the south east region, they were also awarded by MK Food and Leisure "Long standing restaurant of the year".

Popular with visiting actors and actresses appearing at the nearby theatre speaks volumes for both service and food.

As a family owned restaurant Ali and his brothers are keen to impress visiting diners that the food is both imaginative and flavoursome and with over 30 dishes to choose from you are spoilt for choice.

All these dishes are freshly prepared by Ali's three highly skilled chefs using as much local produce as can be sourced.

Always popular is the Rajdhani buffet, held on both Sunday and Monday evenings and with over 25 items on offer there's always something for everyone.

In a rush? Why not enjoy a fabulous take-away, which on orders over £12 is delivered free, or if you would rather collect, Ali is quite happy to give you a 20% off any order over £15.00 (excluding set menus and Thali dishes).

Why not take advantage of a massive 25% off your total food bill when dining in the restaurant by simply presenting the Rajdhani Special Foodie Voucher found at the back of this guide? (See voucher for details).

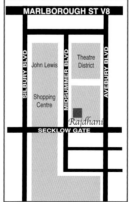

Opening times: Open 7 days a week
Mon-Thur 12.00 pm - 2.30 pm & 6.00 pm - 11.00 pm
Fri 6.00 pm - 12.00 am
Sat 12.00 pm - 2.30 pm & 6.00 pm - 12.00 am
Sun 12.00 pm - 10.30 pm

THE CARRINGTON ARMS

Cranfield Road
Moulsoe
Newport Pagnell
Buckinghamshire MK16 0HB
Tel: 01908 218050
Fax: 01908 217850
Email: enquiries@thecarringtonarms.co.uk
www.thecarringtonarms.co.uk

The Carrington Arms is an imposing 19th century listed building only one mile from junction 14 of the M1 in the picturesque village of Moulsoe.

For over 20 years The Carrington Arms has been famous for steaks using 21 Day Aged Bedfordshire Beef, served from a butchers counter in their open kitchen and the current owners (The Dodman Family) carry on this tradition. More recently it has been selected in 'The Independent' newspaper in their top 50. The reviewer said, "they have one of the most delicious items of food I have eaten in Britain, which is the steak marinated in Jack Daniels".

Alongside their counter they have introduced a restaurant à la carte and a bar menu using the best in fresh local ingredients. They are immensely proud of the local produce they use, especially their meat, game and poultry with herbs and salads from their own garden. They also source local real ales from micro breweries in Cranfield, Olney and Silverstone.

The Carrington is revisiting our recent culinary past for their à la carte. Dishes with names which will be familiar to all of us such as; Prawn Cocktail, Kedgeree, Duck Club Sandwich, Roast Pork and Apple Sauce, Raspberry Ripple and Rocky Road. But in the hands of the Carrington's Team expect their innovation and unique style to put their mark on these classics. They also now serve Breakfast and Weekend Brunch, making The Carrington Arms a true all day venue.

There are sixteen en suite chalet style bedrooms within the gardens, each with a flat screen television, free Wi-Fi, and tea and coffee facilities.

THE FOODIE GUIDE
Diner Review

"Wonderful fresh food and great service, will definitely be returning here."

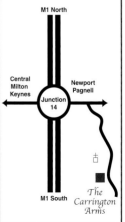

M1 North

Central Milton Keynes — Junction 14 — Newport Pagnell

M1 South

The Carrington Arms

Food service times:
Breakfast Mon-Fri 7.30 am - 9.30 am
Weekend Brunch Sat & Sun 8.00 am - 12.00 pm
Mon-Sat 12.00 pm - 10.00 pm
Sun 12.00 pm - 9.30 pm

Red Lion
COUNTRY HOTEL

Wavendon Road, Salford, Milton Keynes MK17 8AZ
Tel: 01908 583117
Email: info@redlionhotel.eu
www.redlionhotel.eu

THE FOODIE GUIDE
Diner Review
"Great welcoming country pub and tasty traditional fare."

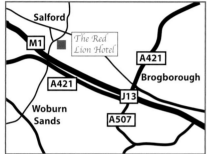

The Red Lion in Salford Village has been in the hands of Bob and Pauline Sapsford for 23 years and has in that time been a pub/restaurant that has consistently delivered a friendly, traditional pub/dining experience.

It's a traditional country inn with log fires, a huge beer garden and six letting rooms. Recently refurbished with a fresh new look but has managed to keep its cosy country pub feel.

The extensive menu has something to suit all tastes, occasions and budgets with top quality steak meals, seafood and chicken dishes alongside a great selection of light meals and snacks. There are spicy and classic dishes and a fair selection for vegetarians too. And for wine and ale lovers they have achieved 'Wine Pub of the Year' awards nationaly and locally with Charles Wells and have been in the Good Beer Guide for 20 years.

Food service times:
Mon-Sat 12.00 pm - 2.00 pm & 6.30 pm - 10.00 pm
Sun 12.00 pm - 2.30 pm & 6.30 pm - 9.00 pm

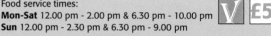

Voongs

1-2 Woodward House
Cambridge Street
Bletchley
MK2 2TH
Tel: 01908 370292
www.voongs.co.uk

You must try it to believe it.

Food service times:
Mon Closed all day Monday
Tue-Fri 12.00 pm - 2.00 pm & 6.00 pm - 10.00 pm
Sat 6.00 pm - 10.00 pm
Sun 12.00 pm - 2.00 pm (Special Buffet)

£5

THE FOODIE GUIDE
Diner Review
"This is my favourite - welcoming and extremely good food."

George Street
Woburn
Bedfordshire
MK17 9PX
Tel: 01525 290441
Fax: 01525 290432
Email: inn@woburn.co.uk
www.woburn.co.uk

Two AA rosettes
for fine food

Olivier's Restaurant takes its name from Executive Chef Olivier Bertho. Having trained and worked in his native France before coming to work in England, he has been at the helm of Olivier's for 11 years and is justifiably proud that the restaurant holds The Foodie Guide Award for Bedfordshire 2010, 2011 and 2012 in addition to holding 2 AA Rosettes.

Olivier's Restaurant offers a stylish setting and friendly ambiance to enjoy the very best of contemporary English and continental dining. For Olivier, the menus are very much a collaboration of ideas from his team of chefs and Sous Chef Ben King.

The menus are complemented by a well stocked cellar with a wine list from around the globe. The restaurant also offers a range of daily specials and often celebrates special occasions with one-off dishes for lunch or dinner. However, it is Olivier's passion for food and ultimate aim to offer guests a wonderfully planned menu, using great quality produce throughout the seasons that continues to inspire him.

THE FOODIE GUIDE
Diner Review

"The food is absolutely delicious and the staff are very professional and courteous."

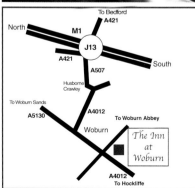

The Inn
at
Woburn

Food service times:
Mon - Sat Lunch: 12.00 pm - 2.00 pm Dinner: 6.30 pm - 9.30 pm
Sun Lunch: 12.30 pm - 2.00 pm Dinner: 6.30 pm - 9.30 pm Afternoon Tea: 3.00 pm - 5.30 pm

Voucher valid Mon - Sat off à la carte only

Bedfordshire **eating out** Bedfordshire

ST. HELENA
RESTAURANT

High Street
Elstow
Bedfordshire
MK42 9XP
Tel: 01234 344848
www.sthelenarestaurant.co.uk

THE FOODIE AWARD
2013
Bedfordshire
winner
as voted by
THE FOODIE GUIDE readers

St Helena is set in what was the birth village of the famous Christian writer John Bunyan. Converted from a private 17th century house it sits in a lovely walled garden not far from Elstow's picturesque village green.

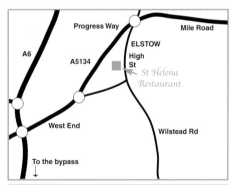

Four separate dining areas greet you upon entering through the garden, culminating in a contemporary garden room. Beyond this can be found a small walled seating area heavily scented in the summer with fragrant roses, lavender, honeysuckle and rosemary. Fine paintings, beautiful mirrors and antiques give the interior a tranquil and peaceful feel during quiet midweek periods with a much busier feel at the weekend.

Now after 25 yrs of working together with more or less the same brigade Raffaele and Franco are pleased to introduce new Head Chef and 2011 Professional Masterchef Finalist Steve Barringer to the team. Steve brings with him his own individual style gleaned from working at some of the most respected restaurants in the country and alongside some highly talented chefs. His style and philosophy is centred around an eclectic interpretation of classic and modern dishes, the emphasis being on freshness and interesting combinations. The end result being visually pleasing with a spectrum of flavours tantalising the palate but with a certain lightness of touch that hopefully leaves you wanting more. His food is not tummy filling but it is tummy pleasing! His menus change at will..... once he believes a dish has been "mastered" he likes to move onto new and fresh avenues of today's "food culture". He is a very young and talented chef but along with his classical training and modern approach to food we believe he has a wonderful future in our industry !

Food service times:
Sunday & Monday Closed all day
Tue 7.00 pm - 9.00 pm (last orders)
Wed-Thur 12.15 pm - 1.00 pm (last orders)
& 7.00 pm - 9.00 pm (last orders)
Fri-Sat 7.00 pm - 9.00 pm (last orders)

THE FOODIE AWARD
2008
winner

lunch   dinner

THE FOODIE GUIDE
Diner Review

"This restaurant has everything you could ever hope for....and much, much more! Not only is the food totally amazing there is a wine list to match!"

The Three Tuns

57 Main Road
Biddenham
Bedfordshire
MK40 4BD
Tel: 01234 354847
Email: info@thethreetunsbiddenham.co.uk
www.thethreetunsbiddenham.co.uk

THE FOODIE GUIDE
Diner Review

"Brilliant food and service, definitely worth travelling to this one."

Situated in the beautiful backwater which is Biddenham, the Three Tuns has recently undergone an extensive refurbishment including a 50 seater extension, by new owner/chef Chris Smith. Trained by the late Peter Chandler of Paris House, Chris then spent a number of years working alongside Jean Christophe Novelli progressing further by gaining 2 AA Rosettes in 2010.

Chris is passionate when it comes to sourcing the very best in seasonal produce with much supplied locally. Everything from sauces to ice cream is prepared on site. Adapting many traditional dishes to fit the modern English menu and with an excellent choice of daily specials and bar meals there is something for everyone.

Food service times:
Mon - Sat 12.00 pm - 2.30 pm & 6.00 pm - 9.30 pm
Sun 12.00 pm - 4.00 pm
Bar is open Monday to Sunday 12.00 pm - 11.30 pm

The Kings Head

Ivinghoe
Leighton Buzzard
Bedfordshire
LU7 9EB
Tel: 01296 668388
Fax: 01296 668107
Email: info@kingsheadivinghoe.co.uk
www.kingsheadivinghoe.co.uk

THE FOODIE GUIDE
Diner Review

"The food here is creative and always top quality taste."

The Kings Head is situated in the very heart of the picturesque village of Ivinghoe, on the Beds, Bucks and Herts borders. This ivy covered building dates back to times when quality and service went hand in hand and happily it still exists here to this day.

We pride ourselves on good old fashioned service and serious professionalism. Georges de Maison's passion for quality food, meticulous attention to detail and impeccable service ensures that your dining experience will be memorable if not unique. Soft candlelight and shimmering silverware complement the restaurants already inviting ambience.

Chef de Cuisine Jonathan O'Keeffe is famed for his skillfully prepared eclectic menus. Only the very best and freshest of produce is used with much of this sourced locally. After lunch or perhaps before dinner, why not take a stroll around the village and visit the windmill. If the weather is inclement take the opportunity sit back in one of our comfy chairs, order your favourite aperitif and let the world go by! Alternatively, take a few moments to explore over 50 original works of art which adorn the walls.

A Banqueting Suite is available for conferences and private dining for up to 40 guests. For larger functions and weddings, marquees can be put in the beautiful walled garden.

We promise a warm welcome and look forward to seeing you soon.

Vouchers valid Mon-Thur for dinner only 10% DC

Food service times:
Mon-Sat 12.00 pm - 2.15 pm & 7.00 pm - 9.15 pm
Sun 12.00 pm - 2.15 pm

Galloway's

Aberdeen House
22-23 Market Place
Woburn
Bedfordshire
MK17 9PZ
Tel: 01525 290496
www.gallowayswoburn.com

THE FOODIE GUIDE
Diner Review

"The food is delicious here, presented well and the service is perfect."

'Party bookings and pre-booked lunches are welcomed'

Galloway's is a family run restaurant providing a relaxed informal atmosphere in a Grade II listed building in the heart of the historic village of Woburn.

Tuesday is our Pasta, Steak and Fish evening and Wednesday to Saturday we offer an à la carte menu which changes regularly, using only the best fresh produce. On Sunday we add our traditional roast selection to the menu for lunchtime service and we always have delicious vegetarian dishes.

Open for Lunch and Dinner service during December. We will be celebrating our 18th Anniversary in November.

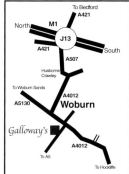

Food service times:
Tue-Sat 6.30 pm - 10.00 pm (last orders)
Sun 12.00 pm - 3.00 pm

DC

The Prince of Wales

24 Bedford Street, Ampthill, Bedfordshire MK45 2NB
Tel: 01525 840504
Fax: 01525 840574
Email: ricksbar1@aol.com
www.princeofwales-ampthill.com

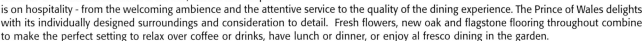

THE FOODIE GUIDE
Diner Review

"Relaxing surroundings, efficient service and very good fresh food."

Welcome to the Prince of Wales, where freshly prepared quality food and wines meets informality and a relaxing atmosphere in a unique but comfortable setting. The Prince of Wales is a traditional red brick town inn, where the emphasis is on hospitality - from the welcoming ambience and the attentive service to the quality of the dining experience. The Prince of Wales delights with its individually designed surroundings and consideration to detail. Fresh flowers, new oak and flagstone flooring throughout combine to make the perfect setting to relax over coffee or drinks, have lunch or dinner, or enjoy al fresco dining in the garden.

The award winning Prince of Wales has now been included nationally in The Good Pub Guide for the past four years including 2012. We pride ourselves on only using the finest locally sourced produce which is lovingly prepared daily by our team of experienced chefs.

Families with children are welcome at any time of the week and depending on what they eat we charge accordingly. Food allergies are taken very seriously by the chefs at The Prince of Wales, we can cater for gluten, nut and lactose free. Please advise us upon booking and we will accommodate all your dietary requirements. We are also dog friendly so after a long walk in Ampthill Park you can rest and enjoy a meal in our welcoming bar with your dog. Free Wi-Fi available and you can also find us on Facebook.

The Prince of Wales has the perfect atmosphere for every occasion. Private parties of up to 100 people are catered for, the restaurant is ideal for wedding receptions, banquets, parties or any special occasion. Alternatively, we also offer outside catering. We look forward to welcoming you at The Prince of Wales.

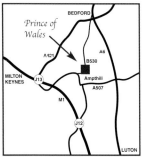

Opening times:
Mon-Fri 9.00 am - 11.00 pm
Sat 9.00 am - midnight
Sun 12.00 pm - 8.00 pm
Thursday night is steak night. Sunday lunch 2 courses: £16.50, 3 courses: £18.50.

Vouchers valid Monday to Thursday evenings only

DC £5 10%

Bedfordshire **eating out** Bedfordshire

Chez Jerome

26 Church Street
Dunstable
Bedfordshire
LU5 4RU
Tel: 01582 603310
Email: info@chezjerome.co.uk
www.chezjerome.co.uk

THE FOODIE GUIDE
Diner Review
"Traditional French dishes with a modern twist, excellent!"

Chez Jerome is owned and run by husband and wife team Jerome and Lina Dehoux. Situated in Dunstable this French restaurant is renound for it's impressive dishes. Head chef Jerome has worked in kitchens all over the world including Switzerland, Luxembourg as well as his native France where he was sous chef in the Michelin star "La Toque Blanche".

The 15th century timber framed building together with its décor certainly sets the mood for experiencing Jerome's superb skill as a chef. Most of his ingredients he sources locally, its freshness and quality is apparent in the taste. The layout of the restaurant is ideal and even allows for small closed off areas where diners can feel secluded.

With ample parking a few steps away and friendly, knowledgeable staff serving first rate dishes ensures Chez Jerome's ongoing popularity and a really nice touch is that they will open early for you if you wish to eat before going to the theatre or cinema.

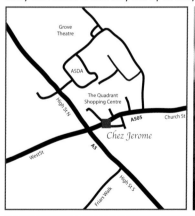

Food service times:
Tue-Fri 12.00 pm - 2.30 pm & 6.00 pm - 10.00 pm
Sat 12.00 pm - 2.30 pm & 6.00 pm - 10.30 pm
Sun 12.00 pm - 3.00 pm
Mon (December only) 12.00 pm - 2.30 pm & 6.00 pm - 10.00 pm

Martins Pond

The Green
Potten End
Berkhamsted
Hertfordshire HP4 2QQ
Tel: 01442 864318
www.martinspond.com

Melanie, Neil, Daniel and the team warmly welcome you to 'Martins Pond', a family owned and run pub restaurant.

As valued guests to our home we aim to exceed your expectations in the delivery of everything, from good food to the ale, the wine to the service, all within a relaxed and informal atmosphere. Being passionate about our business we endeavour to source the best quality produce and have selected local suppliers to ensure outstanding results.

All of our meat is freshly delivered three times a week by 'H G Strattons' a third generation family butchers with 65 years experience who source and retail superior grade produce from a range of trusted suppliers. Our fresh fish is supplied by 'Lovely Lee' a small Watford based fishmongers who deliver each day, direct from Billingsgate market. Finally, all our fresh fruit and vegetables are delivered twice a week from 'R Harris & Sons', a family run greengrocers who live just down the road from us.

Our amazingly talented young head chef Andy Mayersbeth has an uncompromising commitment to flavour and quality, using these fine, fresh ingredients to ensure your meal looks and tastes superb.

As well as fantastic fresh food we also have on offer a diverse range of beverages, from the hand selected wine list from 'R & N Chateaux Wines' which covers a wide choice of old and new world wines to tempt every palette, to our well kept real ales such as London Pride. We have also started to supply ale from 'Red Squirrel' one of the most awarded breweries in Hertfordshire, which is right on the borders of the village. All our ales are nurtured with tender loving care to deliver a visually bright, aromatic beer that tastes clean and fresh.

We hope you enjoy our cuisine and if there is anything we can do to enhance your dining experience please let us know.

THE FOODIE GUIDE
Diner Review

"We had a delicious lunch here, combined with a country walk... perfect!"

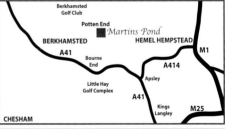

Opening times:
Mon-Sat 12.00 pm - 11.00 pm
Sun 12.00 pm - 4.00 pm

  Please quote voucher use when booking

Food service times:
Mon-Sat 12.00 pm - 2.30 pm & 6.00 pm - 9.00 pm
Sun 12.00 pm - 4.00 pm
Open Christmas Day, Closed Boxing Day

18TH CENTURY COUNTRY INN & RESTAURANT

Hog Pits Bottom
Flaunden
Hemel Hempstead
Hertfordshire
HP3 0PH
Tel: 01442 833322
Email: goodfood@bricklayersarms.com
www.bricklayersarms.com

"Hertfordshire's Restaurant of the Year 2006, 2009, 2010, 2011, 2012 & 2013" – "The Foodie Guide"
AA Best Herts Pub "AA Pick of the Pubs 2013"
Herts Dining Pub of the Year "The Good Pub Guide"
Michelin Guide 2013
Freehouse of The Year & Food Pub of The Year - "Publican Magazines Regional Winner"

THE FOODIE GUIDE
Diner Review

"The food, service and atmosphere is always fantastic, just perfect!"

The Bricklayers Arms is an 18th century, ivy clad and flint built listed building, tucked away in the tiny Hertfordshire village of Flaunden which can be found at the end of the winding lanes that snake between Chipperfield and Latimer.

A picturesque pub in a beautiful location often featured in film and tv series. You are sure to receive a warm welcome from one of the Michaels family where you can enjoy the atmosphere with the pubs low wooden beams and real log fire.

Over the past five years, The Bricklayers Arms has certainly gained an excellent reputation for its English traditional and French Fusion menu created by its award winning chef, Claude Paillet. You can enjoy the same menu throughout the restaurant and pub seven days a week with dishes ranging at lunchtime from their famous smoked fish plate (all smoked on the premises), home made terrines to their traditional cod in Tring ale batter; 21 day aged fillet Steaks and local fillet of pork bred from Worcestershire black spotted pigs.

You'll always find a selection of fresh fish dishes and vegetarian options on the menu.

Food service times:
Mon-Sat 12.00 pm - 2.30 pm & 6.30 pm - 9.30 pm
Sun 12.00 pm - 3.30 pm & 6.30 pm - 8.30 pm

 £5

Hertfordshire **eating out** *Hertfordshire*

CHEZ MUMTAJ

Modern French-Asian Dining
Restaurant & Saffron Lounge Champagne Bar

136-142 London Road
St Albans
Hertfordshire
AL1 1PQ
Tel: 01727 800033
Email: info@chezmumtaj.com
www.chezmumtaj.com

THE FOODIE GUIDE
Diner Review

"Extremely flavoursome dishes and amazing presentation."

Winner of St. Albans Retailer of The Year 2011
Winner of St. Albans Best Restaurant of The Year 2011
Top Ten AA Rosette Academy's Hall of Fame Award
Top 4 Best in Britain Award by Mood Food Magazine 2011
Independent Newspaper Top Ten Best Asian Restaurant 2010-2011

Chez Mumtaj is designed to impart the essence of stunning French and Asian cuisine, showcasing evolved modern dishes from India, France, Thailand, China and Malaysia for the discerning palate. The philosophy at Chez Mumtaj is to be innovative, progressive, persistent and passionate with cuisine and service.

Award winning Executive Chef Chad Rahman has created an eclectic menu depicting a diversity of traditional dishes with a contemporary twist. The menu encompasses a wide range of tastes and flavours journeying through South East Asia and Europe incorporating nuances of Pan Asian and European cuisines. Menus change regularly using only the finest and freshest seasonal ingredients.

For private or corporate events of 8 to 16 guests, there is a private dining room. They can co-ordinate and create a menu to suit your requirements so that the event is successful, bringing attention to detail, care and hospitality. The aim is to create a unique and memorable experience, tailored to your needs.

The Saffron Lounge offers an ideal space for pre-luncheon and dinner drinks and an Asian Tapas Bar Food Menu. The lounge can accommodate up to 28 guests seated and 50 for cocktails. The Saffron Lounge echoes many of the charming characteristics of the restaurant with rich mahogany panelled walls, luxurious leather banquette seating and antique mirror-panelled walls and in-built booths for privacy.

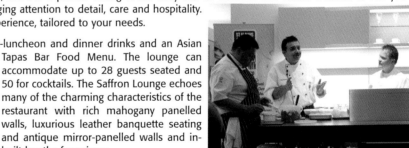

Chad Rahman (centre) at cookery demonstration

Voucher not valid Friday to Saturday.
Accepted from à la carte menu only.
Minimum of 2 courses (Starter & Main)

£5

Food service times:
Tue-Sun 12.00 pm - 2.30 pm & 6.00 pm - 11.00 pm
The Saffron Lounge opening times:
Tue-Sun 6.00 pm - 11.00 pm

THE ALFORD ARMS

Frithsden
Nr Hemel Hempstead
Hertfordshire
HP1 3DD
Tel: 01442 864480
Fax: 01442 876893
Email: info@alfordarmsfrithsden.co.uk
www.alfordarmsfrithsden.co.uk

Set in the unruffled hamlet of Frithsden, nr. Berkhamsted and surrounded by National Trust woodland, The Alford Arms is a pretty Victorian pub, full of surprises. The flower filled terrace overlooks the village green, a haven of tranquillity and historic Ashridge forest is right on our doorstep.

Step inside and you can't help but get caught up in the lively, warm atmosphere, where Zoffany fabrics and antique artwork set the mood. Wooden tables and chairs gleaned from nearby auctions add the tone and an open fire stands ready.

Push past the merry throng frothing at the bar and the elegant freshness of the dining room is revealed. The ying and yang of the modern, essential pub: down-home cheer in the front and refined dining in the back. It's best to book of course, but if you haven't there's rarely a chance of you leaving hungry - the Alford's jolly crew would scarce allow it. Always a pub first and foremost, there is something for everyone, which hopefully will justify the effort of trying to find us! Your mobile may not have a signal, but free wifi will provide a soothing umbilical to the world outside.

The award winning seasonal menu and daily specials balance originality along with more classic fare and we are firm believers in using local produce wherever possible. So whether you want a slap up meal with top-notch wine, a few pints with your mates or just space to watch the world go by, you will always feel welcome.

Opening times:
Mon - Sat 11.00 am - 11.00 pm
Sun 12.00 pm - 10.30 pm
Food service times:
Mon - Thur 12.00 pm - 2.30 pm & 6.30 pm - 9.30 pm
Fri 12.00 pm - 2.30 pm & 6.30 pm - 10.00 pm
Sat 12.00 pm - 3.00 pm & 6.30 pm - 10.00 pm
Sun 12.00 pm - 4.00 pm & 6.30 pm - 9.30 pm

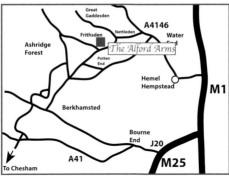

The Alford Arms

THE FOODIE GUIDE
Diner Review

"Perfect for a drive out into the countryside. You must try the Bubble & Squeak."

The Fox & Hounds

2 High Street
Hunsdon
Ware
Hertfordshire
SG12 8NH
Tel: 01279 843999
Email: info@foxandhounds-hunsdon.co.uk
www.foxandhounds-hunsdon.co.uk

THE FOODIE GUIDE
Diner Review

"We decided to travel out to this place and were very pleased we did, the food was excellent and imaginative."

Featured in Michelin Guide 2013, Good Food Guide 2013, AA Good Pub Guide Pick of the Pubs 2013, AA Britains Best Pubs, Hardens 2013, Sunday Telegraph Stella magazine June 2013.

The Fox & Hounds is a family run establishment in the pretty village of Hunsdon. It is established as one of Hertfordshire's leading pub & dining room, receiving impressive reviews and accolades in numerous press articles and guides. Chef/proprietor James Rix has previously worked in some of London's most celebrated eateries.

Everything is made in-house and the menu changes daily making the best of good quality seasonal produce. Rare breed meats and locally shot game feature and seafood is delivered daily from the East and South coasts. Sample dishes include Black Pudding from Normandy and a Fried Duck Egg, Palourde Clams, Chorizo and Sherry for starters. For main course why not try the popular Cote de Boeuf, Sauce Béarnaise and Hand Cut Chips or Calfs Liver Persillade and Duck Fat Potato Cake. Finish off with Chocolate Pot, Crème Fraiche and Hazelnut Praline, Apple Tart Fine and Salted Caramel Ice Cream. There is an interesting wine list with a good selection offered by the glass or carafe. You will also find an excellent value midweek set menu.

The pub has a friendly, informal atmosphere with a comfy laid back bar, log fire, leather sofas and local ales. The homely dining room features a chandelier and is popular for gatherings of families and friends and for private functions.

The large garden comes into its own in the summer with a large covered/heated patio and children's play area - great to keep the children entertained whilst having a quiet drink or bite to eat.

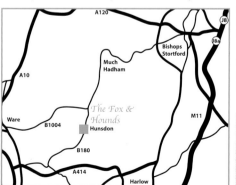

Food service times:
Tue - Sat 12.00 pm - 2.30 pm & 6.00 pm - 9.30 pm
Sun 12.00 pm - 2.30 pm

the rose & crown

YARDLEY HASTINGS

4 Northampton Road
Yardley Hastings
Northamptonshire
NN7 1EX
Tel: 01604 696276
Email: info@roseandcrownbistro.co.uk
www.roseandcrownbistro.co.uk

WINNER
NORTHAMPTONSHIRE
FOOD & DRINK AWARDS 2011/12
PUB OR BAR RESTAURANT OF THE YEAR

Whether it's dining in our bistro, attending one of our events or just relaxing with a glass of wine in the garden you are sure of a warm welcome.

The Rose & Crown captures all the qualities of what a classic English country pub should be. Great real ales, carefully selected wines, real food at pub prices and an attention to detail including a daily changing menu, free newspapers to relax over your beer, fresh flowers, fantastic coffee and most importantly of all – a high level of service to make it a memorable visit.

Andrew and Melissa are passionate about food and drink and have created the Bistro which blends traditional British cuisine with a worldly flair having had many years experience in the industry.

We have regular live music events from jazz to rock and blues and are able to host dinner bookings of up to 70.

THE FOODIE GUIDE
Diner Review

"What a fantastic place to eat, the food and atmosphere is perfect."

The Rose & Crown Bistro

A428
To Northampton
Northampton Rd
High St
Yardley Hastings
A428
Chase Park Rd
To Bedford
B5388

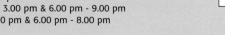

Food service times:
Mon 6.00 pm - 9.00 pm
Tue-Sat 12.00 pm - 3.00 pm & 6.00 pm - 9.00 pm
Sun 12.00 pm - 3.00 pm & 6.00 pm - 8.00 pm

Murrays
AT WHITTLEBURY HALL

Whittlebury Hall Hotel & Spa
Whittlebury
Nr Towcester
Northamptonshire
NN12 8QH
Tel: 0845 400 0001
Fax: 01327 857867
Email: reservations@whittleburyhall.co.uk
www.whittleburyhall.co.uk

Two AA rosettes
for fine food

Murrays provides a relaxing venue to enjoy the creative dishes presented by our award winning Chef and his brigade.

Discover fine dining with a difference. Boasting two AA Rosettes and an intimate and relaxing atmosphere, Murrays provides the perfect setting for our award-winning Head Chef and his brigade, to introduce you to his Modern British Menu.

Food service times:
Tue - Sat 7.00 pm - 9.30 pm

To begin - BEETROOT BAVAROIS
Beetroot, Goats Curd & Walnuts

The creative dishes that our Head Chef and team presents have classical and international influences and the Murrays menu changes regularly providing guests with the opportunity to taste the latest blends of flavours and ingredients to make your visit truly memorable. The restaurant also offers a Tasting Menu giving you the opportunity to try some of the most delicious dishes created by our professional team.

As the name suggests, Murrays is a homage to the legendary F1 commentator Murray Walker and whilst you relax in the lounge and during dinner you can reminisce by viewing the collection of photographs with F1 celebrities and some unique anecdotes of his memorable career.

For more details and menus, visit www.whittleburyhall.co.uk or call us to book your fine dining experience on 0845 400 0001.

Main dish - GUINEA FOWL
Truffles, Figs, Pancetta & Lemon

THE FOODIE GUIDE
Diner Review
"The food here not only looks like a work of art, but tastes absolutely delicious, it's apparent how much work goes into every creation."

To finish - ETON MESS
Meringue, Strawberry Sorbet & Strawberries

The Vine House
Hotel & Restaurant

100 High Street, Paulerspury
Northamptonshire, NN12 7NA
Tel: 01327 811267
Email: info@vinehousehotel.com
www.vinehousehotel.com

THE FOODIE AWARD
2013
Northamptonshire
winner
as voted by
THE FOODIE GUIDE readers

THE FOODIE GUIDE
Diner Review
"This is my favourite, the food is superb every time."

Quality Food, Service and Setting

Dedicated Foodies Chef Marcus and Host Julie Springett love sharing all that is great about their multi award winning restaurant with rooms above. Attending to every detail whilst honouring the centuries old restored building, they refresh and move with the times, striving always to deliver top quality food, great service and a welcoming setting. Located just off the A5 at Paulerspury, near Silverstone home of motor racing, Towcester for horse racing, county towns Northampton and Buckingham, shoppers' havens Milton Keynes and Bicester Village, this is considered something of a hidden gem.

Here it really is all about the food. Passionately presented, packed with flavour and interesting marriages that really work for affordable top taste experiences whatever the season. Locally sourced ingredients including rare breed meats, day boat caught fish, flora from the cottage garden and much more excite the taste buds. When Marcus works his magic these found a fusion of traditional English and modern continental cuisine with a twist. From only £30.95 for 3 courses, £27.50 for 2 courses per head, expect informal dining with crisp linen table cloths and award winning food.

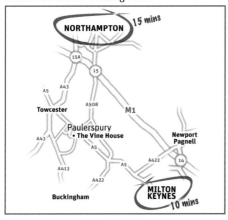

Food service times:
Lunch **Tue-Sat** 12.30 pm - 1.45 pm
Dinner **Mon-Sun** 6.30 pm - 10.00 pm
Special openings on Sunday for events and
stopovers / residents

£5

Northampton Road
Grafton Regis
Northamptonshire
NN12 7SR
Tel: 01908 542123
www.pubgraftonregis.co.uk

THE FOODIE GUIDE
Diner Review

"The food here is a pure delight. The fresh fish is always a good choice."

The White Hart is a stone under thatch 16th Century building located in the small village of Grafton Regis and has been owned by the Drake family for over 17 years.

Owner chef Alan and his team prepare all their dishes on the premises freshly and daily. The menu changes frequently depending on what fresh produce is currently available. The fish arrives daily from Grimsby supplied by Keith Wright who delivers fresh fish in the area, providing a friendly door to door service for many villages. The meat which is mainly British is supplied by Bookers of Great Billing. Alan's insistence for using only the freshest ingredients possible ensures an ever changing menu, therefore the Specials Board changes daily.

Andy takes care of front of house and is constantly trying to improve on what they have. The concept at the pub now offers one large menu in all areas so you can enjoy your meal in the air conditioned restaurant or in the traditional lounge bar area and weather permitting their wonderful garden which has a large patio area.

Having this much commitment brings rewards having been awarded by Green King Brewery the title of "Catering Pub of the Year" winning first place from over 700 other entrants. Little wonder then that their board outside thanks over 21,000 diners that have visited them this past year.

As you would imagine, the restaurant is very popular, comfortably seating between 26 and 29 so you are strongly advised to book your table to avoid disappointment, and for that special occasion you can book the entire restaurant providing the numbers are a minimum of 24.

Food service times:
Mon Closed
Tue-Sat 12.00 pm - 2.00 pm & 6.00 pm - 9.30 pm
Sun 12.00 pm - 2.00 pm & 7.00 pm - 9.00 pm

Vouchers accepted Tue-Thurs only

Bar Restaurant

Northamptonshire **eating out**

CROMWELL COTTAGE

1 High Street
Kislingbury
Northamptonshire
NN7 4AG
Tel: 01064 830288
www.thecromwellcottagekislingbury.co.uk

Before word got around, the Cromwell Cottage was one of Kislingbury's best-kept secrets. The cosy pub and restaurant serves well kept cask ales, quaffable wines and tasty, unpretentious pub food, lovingly prepared by local chef Jules.

The beautifully restored building was once known as 'the restaurant over the bridge' and has played host to various shenanigans over the years, most notably when Oliver Cromwell used it as a hideout from marauding Royalists.

Food served all day:
Mon-Sat 11.30 am - 10.00 pm
Sun 11.30 am - 9.30 pm

Opening times:
Mon-Sat 9.30 am (for tea & coffee) - 11.00 pm
Sun 9.30 am (for tea & coffee) - 10.30 pm

THE FOODIE GUIDE
Diner Review
"Nice atmosphere, good service and delicious fare on offer."

THE OLD CROWN

1 Stoke Road
Ashton
Northampton
Northamptonshire
NN7 2JN
Tel: 01604 862268
Email: bex@theoldcrownashton.co.uk
www.theoldcrownashton.co.uk

THE FOODIE GUIDE
Diner Review

"Welcoming service and great British food."

The small village of Ashton is just a stones throw from the A508 midway between Northampton and Milton Keynes. Chef Ian and his wife Bex took over this lovely dining pub just a couple of years ago and have already made massive changes, which include new menus as well as good ales. Not surprising then that their reputation for good food is gradually spreading further afield.

The Old Crown is the heart of the village and is a warm and welcoming inn with a lovely safe garden to relax in the summer sunshine. Winter times the cosy interior is a great place to just sit back and watch the world go by.

As a chef and owner Ian ensures that all his produce is sourced locally wherever possible and meals prepared freshly in his kitchen. He sets high standards and expects his kitchen team to maintain them. You can expect a good choice from the menu that changes regularly. Starters such as Fresh Crab with a Sweet Pepper Ketchup and Sautéed Chicken Livers Brandy and Bacon accompany main courses that may include

Rump Steak with Homemade Chips and Mustard Sauce, Braised Beef Cheeks with Beetroot Risotto and Salmon Fillet with Braised Fennel and Chickpeas. They also offer a choice of roasts on Sundays and specials daily.

Front of house, wife Bex is there to welcome you and ensure your visit is a memorable one. All well-behaved dogs are also very welcome.

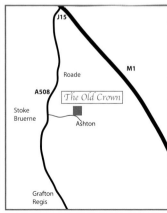

Opening times:
Tue-Fri 12.00 pm to 3.00 pm & 6.00 pm - 11.30 pm
Sat 12.00 pm - 11.30 pm
Sun 12.00 pm - 10.30 pm

Food service times:
Tue-Fri 12.00 pm - 3.00 pm & 6.00 pm - 9.30 pm
Sat 12.00 pm - 9.30 pm
Sun 12.00 pm - 6.00 pm

30 **The Angel Restaurant**
47 Bicester Road, Long Crendon, Aylesbury, Bucks HP18 9EE
Tel: 01844 208268 Email: info@angelrestaurant.co.uk
www.angelrestaurant.co.uk

31 # Auberge du Lac
Brocket Hall
Welwyn
Hertfordshire
AL8 7XG
Tel: 01707 368888
Email: aubergeevents@brocket-hall.co.uk
www.aubergedulac.co.uk

---

32 **The Barge Inn**
15 Newport Road, Woolstone, Milton Keynes MK15 0AE
Tel: 01908 233841
www.vintageinn.co.uk

---

33 **The Bedford Arms**
High Street, Oakley, Beds MK43 7RH
Tel: 01234 822280
www.bedfordarmsoakley.co.uk

---

34 **The Bell & Bear**
12 High Street, Emberton, Bucks MK46 5DH
Tel: 01234 711565 **Email:** hello@bellandbear.net
www.bellandbear.net

---

35 **The Bell Hotel & Inn**
21 Bedford Street, Woburn, Beds MK17 9QB
Tel: 01525 290280
www.bellinn-woburn.co.uk

---

36 **The Bell Inn**
Main Street, Beachampton, Bucks MK19 6DX
Tel: 01908 563861 **Email:** info@thebellrestaurant.co.uk
www.thebellrestaurant.co.uk

37 # The Birch
20 Newport Road
Woburn
Buckinghamshire
MK17 9HX
Tel: 01525 290295
Email: info@birchwoburn.com
www.birchwoburn.com

---

38 **The Belvedere**
Ardmore House Hotel, 54 Lemsford Road, St Albans, Herts AL1 3PR
Tel: 01727 859313
www.ardmorehousehotel.co.uk

39 # The Black Horse
Ireland
Shefford
Bedfordshire
SG17 5QL
Tel: 01462 811398
Email: info@blackhorseireland.com
www.blackhorseireland.com

---

40 **The Boat Inn**
Stoke Bruerne, Northants, NN12 7SB
Tel: 01604 862428 **Email:** enquiries@boatinn.co.uk
www.boatinn.co.uk

---

41 **The Boot at Sarratt**
The Green, Sarratt, Rickmansworth, Herts WD3 6BL
Tel: 01923 262247 **Email:** thebootsarratt@gmail.com
www.thebootsarratt.com

---

42 **The Brampton Halt**
Pitsford Road, Chapel Brampton, Northants NN6 8BA
Tel: 01604 842676 **Email:** bramptonhalt@mcmanuspub.co.uk
www.mcmanuspub.co.uk

---

43 **Brasserie Blanc**
Chelsea House, 301 Avebury Blvd, Central Milton Keynes, Bucks MK9 2GA
Tel: 01908 546590
www.brasserieblanc.com

---

44 **The Brocket Arms**
Ayot St. Lawrence, Welwyn, Herts AL6 9BT
Tel: 01438 820250 **Email:** bookings@brocketarms.com
www.brocketarms.com

---

45 **The Bull**
Cottered, Buntingford, Nr Stevenage, Herts SG9 9QP
Tel: 01763 281243 **Email:** reservations@thehillside.co.uk
www.thehillside.co.uk

---

46 **The Bull Inn**
9 Market Place, Olney, Bucks MK46 4EA
Tel: 01234 711470 **Email:** thebullolney@gmail.com
www.thebullolney.com

47 **The Chequers Inn**
Kiln Lane, Wooburn Common, Bucks HP10 0JQ
Tel: 01628 529575 **Email:** info@chequers-inn.com
www.chequers-inn.com

48 **The Chequers at Millbrook**
Millbrook, Beds MK45 2JB
Tel: 01525 403835

49 **The Cock Inn**
High Street, Denford, Nr Kettering, Northants NN14 4EQ
Tel: 01832 732565 **Email:** thecockinndenford@gmail.com
www.thecockinndenford.com

50 **The Cock Inn**
16 High Street, North Crawley, Beds MK16 9LH
Tel: 01234 391222 **Email:** info@cockinnnorthcrawley.co.uk
www.cockinnnorthcrawley.co.uk

51 **Cornfields Restaurant**
Wilden Road, Colmworth, Bedfordshire MK44 2NJ
Tel: 01234 378990 **Email:** reservations@cornfieldsrestaurant.co.uk
www.cornfieldsrestaurant.co.uk

52 **The Crooked Chimney**
Cromer Hyde Lane, Lemsford, Welwyn Garden City, Herts AL8 7XE
Tel: 01707 397021
www.vintageinn.co.uk

53 **Dangs**
205 Wellingborough Road, Northampton NN1 4ED
Tel: 01604 607060

54 **Durbar Restaurant**
156 Wellingborough Road, Northampton NN1 4DU
Tel: 01604 604650 **Email:** info@durbar.co.uk
www.durbar.co.uk

55 **Earls Restaurant**
119 Dunstable Street, Ampthill, Beds MK45 2NG
Tel: 01525 404024 **Email:** earlsrestaurant@tiscali.co.uk
www.earlsofampthill.com

56 **The Falcon**
Riverside English Bistro, Rushden Road, Bletsoe, Beds MK44 1QN
Tel: 01234 781222 **Email:** thefalcona6@aol.com
www.thefalconbletsoe.co.uk

57 **Fawsley Hall**
Fawsley, Nr Daventry, Northants NN11 3BA
Tel: 01327 892000 **Email:** info@fawsleyhall.com
www.fawsleyhall.com

58 **The Five Arrows Hotel**
High Street, Waddesdon, Aylesbury, Bucks HP18 0JE
Tel: 01296 651727 **Email:** five.arrows@nationaltrust.org.uk
www.waddesdon.org.uk/five_arrows

59 **The Five Bells**
1 Northill Road, Cople, Beds MK44 3TU
Tel: 01234 838289 **Email:** kilroy@fivebellscople.co.uk
www.fivebellscople.co.uk

60 **Fox and Hounds**
High Street, Riseley, Beds MK44 1DT
Tel: 01234 708240 **Email:** info@foxandhoundsriseley.co.uk

61 **The Fox and Hounds**
Harlestone Road, Lower Harlestone, Northants NN7 4EW
Tel: 01604 821251
www.thefoxandhoundsharlestone.co.uk

62 **The George & Dragon**
Watton-at-Stone, Herts SG14 3TA
Tel: 01920 830285 **Email:** pub@georgeanddragon.co.uk
www.georgeanddragonwatton.co.uk

63 **The Griffin Inn**
25 High Street, Pitsford, Northants NN6 9AD
Tel: 01604 880346
www.griffinpitsford.co.uk

64 **The Hare and Hounds**
The Village, Old Warden, Beds SG18 9HQ
Tel: 01767 627225
www.hareandhoundsoldwarden.co.uk

65
Horse & Jockey
Church End
Ravensden
Bedfordshire MK44 2RR
Tel: 01234 772319
www.horseandjockey.info

Hartwell House & Spa

66 Oxford Road, Nr Aylesbury, Bucks HP17 8NR
Tel: 01296 747444 **Email:** info@hartwell-house.com
www.hartwell-house.com

Jacoby's Bar & Restaurant

67 Churchgate House, 15 West Street, Ware, Herts SG12 9EE
Tel: 01920 469181 **Email:** info@jacobys.co.uk
www.jacobys.co.uk

Just 32

68 32 Sun Street, Hitchin, Herts SG5 1AH
Tel: 01462 455666 **Email:** david@just32.com
www.just32.com

Kashu

69 9 Hatfield Road, St Albans, Herts AL1 3RR
Tel: 01727 854436 **Email:** info@kashu.co.uk
www.kashu.co.uk

La Dolce Vita

70 18 Hopping Hill Gardens, Duston, Northants NN5 6PF
Tel: 01604 580090 **Email:** info@hoppinghare.com
www.hoppinghare.com

La Stalla Restaurant

71 The Green Man, The Green, Clophill, Beds MK45 4AD
Tel: 01525 860352 **Email:** info@lastallarestaurant.co.uk
www.lastallarestaurant.co.uk

Lussmanns

72 Waxhouse Gate, St Albans, Herts AL3 4EW
Tel: 01727 851941 **Email:** chris@lussmanns.com
www.lussmanns.com

The Lytton Arms

73 Park Lane, Old Knebworth, Herts SG3 6QB
Tel: 01438 812312 **Email:** info@lyttonarms.co.uk
www.lyttonarms.co.uk

The Narrow Boat

74 A5 Watling Street, Stowe Hill, Weedon, Northants NN7 4RZ
Tel: 01327 340333
www.narrowboatatweedon.co.uk

The Old Swan

75 58 High Street, Cheddington, Nr Leighton Buzzard, Beds LU7 0RQ
Tel: 01296 668226 **Email:** info@theoldswancheddington.co.uk
www.theoldswancheddington.co.uk

The Oak Restaurant

76 The Pendley Manor Hotel
Cow Lane
Tring, Herts HP23 5QY
Tel: 01442 891891
Email: sales@pendley-manor.co.uk
www.pendley-manor.co.uk

The Old Queens Head

77 Hammersley Lane
Penn
High Wycombe, Bucks
HP10 8EY
Tel: 01494 813371
Email: info@oldqueensheadpenn.co.uk
www.oldqueensheadpenn.co.uk

The Olde Red Lion

78 15 High Street, Kislingbury, Northants NN7 4AQ
Tel: 01604 830219
www.theolderedlion.net

Orangery Restaurant

79 Shendish Manor Hotel & Golf Club, London Rd, Apsley, Herts HP3 0AA
Tel: 01442 232220
www.shendish-manor.com

The Pilgrim

80 25 High Street, North Marston, Bucks MK18 3PD
Tel: 01296 670969 **Email:** info@thepilgrimpub.co.uk
www.thepilgrimpub.co.uk

The Plough Restaurant

81 Kimbolton Road, Bolnhurst, Beds MK44 2EX
Tel: 01234 376274 **Email:** theplough@bolnhurst.com
www.bolnhurst.com

Prego

82 4 High St, Buckingham, MK18 1NT
Tel: 01280 821205 **Email:** mail@pregorestaurants.com
www.pregorestaurants.com

Prego

83 8 St John's St, Newport Pagnell, Bucks, MK16 0EP
Tel: 01908 217535 **Email:** mail@pregorestaurants.com
www.pregorestaurants.com

The Purple Goose
84 61 High Street, Woburn Sands, Bucks MK17 8QY
Tel: 01908 584385 **Email:** mail@thepurplegoose.co.uk
www.thepurplegoose.co.uk

The Red Chilli
85 9 High Street, Buckingham, Bucks MK18 1NT
Tel: 01280 822226
www.redchilligold.com

Redcoats Farmhouse Hotel & Restaurant
86 Redcoats Green, Nr Hitchin, Herts SG4 7JR
Tel: 01438 729500 **Email:** info@redcoats.co.uk
www.redcoats.co.uk

The Red Lion
87 36 Bridle Path, Brafield-on-the-Green, Northants NN7 1BP
Tel: 01604 890707 **Email:** theredlion@mcmanuspub.co.uk
www.theredlionbrafield.co.uk

The Red Lion
88 89 High Street, Yardley Hastings, Northants NN7 1ER
Tel: 01604 696210 **Email:** info@redlionatyardleyhastings.co.uk
www.redliionatyardleyhastings.co.uk

The Red Lion Hotel
89 Main Street, East Haddon, Northants NN6 8BU
Tel: 01604 770223 **Email:** nick@redlioneasthaddon.co.uk
www.redlioneasthaddon.co.uk

Roade House Restaurant & Hotel
90 16 High Street, Roade, Northants NN7 2NW
Tel: 01604 863372 **Email:** info@roadehousehotel.co.uk
www.roadehousehotel.co.uk

The Robin Hood
91 Clifton Reynes, Bucks MK46 5DR
Tel: 01234 711574
www.therobinhoodpub.co.uk

92

The Royal Oak
Frieth Road
Bovingdon Green
Nr Marlow
Bucks SL7 2JF
Tel: 01628 488611
Email: info@royaloakmarlow.co.uk
www.royaloakmarlow.co.uk

The Royal Oak
93 4 Biggleswade Road, Potton, Beds SG19 2LU
Tel: 01767 261888 **Email:** enquiries@theroyaloakpotton.co.uk
www.theroyaloakpotton.co.uk

The Royal Oak at Eydon
94 Lime Avenue, Eydon, Northants NN11 3PG
Tel: 01327 263167
www.theroyaloakateydon.co.uk

The Russell Arms
95 2 Chalkshires Road, Butlers Cross, Ellesborough, Bucks HP17 0TS
Tel: 01296 622618 **Email:** info@therussellarms.com
www.therussellarms.com

The Saracen's Head
96 Main Street, Little Brington, Northants NN7 4HS
Tel: 01604 770640 **Email:** info@yeoldesaracenshead.co.uk
www.thesaracensatbrington.co.uk

The Seafood Café
97 47-49 St Giles Street, Northampton, NN1 1JF
Tel: 01604 627989
www.theseafoodcafe.co.uk

The Silk Road
98 151 Grafton Gate East, Central Milton Keynes, Bucks MK9 1AE
Tel: 01908 200522 **Email:** enquiries@thesilkroadrestaurants.co.uk
www.thesilkroadrestaurants.co.uk

Spaghetti Johns Cafe & Gelateria
99 15 Castle Lane, Bedford, Beds MK40 3NT
Tel: 01234 327323 **Email:** enquiry@spaghettijohns.co.uk
www.spaghettijohns.co.uk

Spice of Bruerne
100 5 The Canalside, Stoke Bruerne, Northants NN12 7SB
Tel: 01604 863330 **Email:** mail@spiceofbruerne.co.uk
www.spiceofbruerne.com

The Stag Inn
101 The Green, Mentmore, Beds LU7 0QF
Tel: 01296 668423 **Email:** info@thestagmentmore.com
www.thestagmentmore.com

St Michaels Manor
102 Fishpool Street, St Albans, Herts AL3 4RY
Tel: 01727 864444
www.stmichaelsmanor.com

103 **The Stuffed Olive**
190 Wellingborough Road, Northampton NN1 4EB
Tel: 01604 631631
www.thestuffedolive.co.uk

104 **The Sun at Northaw**
Judges Hill, Northaw, Potters Bar, Herts EN6 4NL
Tel: 01707 655507   **Email:** info@thesunatnorthaw.co.uk
www.thesunatnorthaw.co.uk

105

The Swan Inn
Village Road
Denham
Bucks
UB9 5BH
Tel: 01895 832085
Email: info@swaninndenham.co.uk
www.swaninndenham.co.uk

106

The Swan
2 Wavendon Road
Salford
Bucks
MK17 8BD
Tel: 01908 281008
Email: swan@peachpubs.com
www.swansalford.co.uk

107 **The Swan at Lamport**
Harborough Road, Lamport, Northants NN6 9EZ
Tel: 01604 686555   **Email:** theswanlamport@mcmanuspub.co.uk
www.theswanlamport.co.uk

108 **The Tree at Cadmore**
Marlow Road, Cadmore End, High Wycombe, Bucks HP14 3PF
Tel: 01494 881183   **Email:** cadmore@treehotel.co.uk
www.cadmore.treehotel.co.uk

109 **The Vanilla Pod**
31 West Street, Marlow, Bucks SL7 2LS
Tel: 01628 898101
www.thevanillapod.co.uk

110 **The Waggon & Horses**
Watling Street, Elstree, Herts WD6 3AA
Tel: 0208 953 1406   **Email:** info@waggonhorses.co.uk
www.waggonhorses.co.uk

111 **The Walnut Tree Inn**
21 Station Road, Blisworth, Northants NN7 3DS
Tel: 01604 859551
www.walnut-tree.co.uk

112 **The Wharf**
Cornhill Lane, Bugbrooke, Northants NN7 3QB
Tel: 01604 832585   **Email:** rich@the-wharf.co.uk
www.the-wharf.co.uk

113 **White Hart**
54 High Street. Flore, Northants NN7 4LW
Tel: 01327 341748
www.whitehartflore.co.uk

114 **White Hart**
Ampthill Road, Maulden, Beds MK45 2DH
Tel: 01525 406118   **Email:** info@whitehartmaulden.com
www.whitehartsaladcart.com

115 **The White Hart**
Brook Lane, Flitton, Beds MK45 5EJ
Tel: 01525 862022   **Email:** philhale@btconnect.com
www.whitehartflitton.co.uk

116 **The White Horse**
White Horse Lane, Burnham Green, Nr Welwyn, Herts AL6 0HA
Tel: 01438 798100
www.whitehorseburnhamgreen.com

117 **The Windhover**
Brampton Lane, Chapel Brampton, Northampton NN6 8AA
Tel: 01604 847859
www.vintageinn.co.uk

118 **The Worlds End**
Ecton, Northants NN6 0QN
Tel: 01604 414521   **Email:** info@theworldsend.org
www.theworldsend.org

119 **Ye Olde Swan**
Newport Road, Woughton on the Green, Milton Keynes, Bucks MK6 3BS
Tel: 01908 679489   **Email:** reza.najafi@pubandkitchenco.com
www.pubandkitchenco.com

120 **The Zodiac Restaurant**
Hanbury Manor Hotel, Ware, Herts SG12 0SD
Tel: 01920 487722
www.marriott.co.uk

121 ARTea Room
Wakefield Country Courtyard, Potterspury, Northants NN12 7QX
Tel: 01327 810245
www.artearoom.co.uk

122 The Barn Restaurant
The Old Dairy Farm Centre, Upper Stowe, Nr Weedon, Northants NN7 4SH
Tel: 01327 349911
www.thebarnrestaurant.net

123 Beckworth Emporium
Glebe Road, Mears Ashby, Northants NN6 0DL
Tel: 01604 812371   **Email:** enquiries@beckworthemporium.co.uk
www.beckworthemporium.co.uk

124 Bluebells Tea Rooms
Lock 39, Startops End, Marsworth, Tring, Herts HP23 4LJ
Tel: 01442 891708

125 Butlers Pantry
10 High Street, Middleton Cheney, Northants OX17 2PB
Tel: 01295 711444

126 The Buttery
Castle Ashby Rural Shopping Yard, Castle Ashby, Northants NN7 1LF
Tel: 01604 696728
www.thebutteryrestaurant.co.uk

127 Canons Ashby Stables Tea Room
Daventry, Northants NN11 3SD
Tel: 01327 860044
www.nationaltrust.org

128 The Courtyard Tea Room
Claydon House, Middle Claydon, Bucks MK18 2EX
Tel: 01296 730004

129 Danesfield House
Henley Road, Marlow-on-Thames, Bucks SL7 2EY
Tel: 01628 891010
www.danesfieldhouse.co.uk

130 Darlingtons Tea Room
Heart of the Shires Shopping Village, A5 Watling St, Nr Weedon NN7 4LB
Tel: 01327 342284

131 Delapre Abbey Tea Room
Delapre Abbey, London Road, Northampton, Northants NN4 8AW
Tel: 01604 708675
www.delapreabbey.org

132 Dreams Coffee Shop
59 St Giles Street, Northampton, Northants NN1 1JF
Tel: 01604 636368

133 Ferny Hill Farm
Ferny Hill, Hadley Wood, Nr Barnet, Herts EN4 0PZ
Tel: 020 8449 3527
www.fernyhillfarm.com

134 Flitwick Manor
Church Road, Flitwick, Beds MK45 1AE
Tel: 01525 712242

135 Halsey's Tea Room
10-11 Market Place, Hitchin, Herts SG5 1DR
Tel: 01462 432023

136 The Hayloft Tea Room
Boycott Farm Shop, Welsh Lane, Stowe, Bucks MK18 5DJ
Tel: 01280 821286
www.boycottfarm.co.uk

137 The Inn at Woburn
George Street, Woburn, Beds MK17 9PX
Tel: 01525 290441
www.theinnatwoburn.com

138 Inn On The Park
Verulamium Park, St. Michaels Street, St Albans, Herts AL3 4SN
Tel: 01727 838246

139 Kelmarsh Hall Tea Room
Kelmarsh, Northants NN6 9LY
Tel: 01604 686543
www.kelmarsh.com

140 Limes Farm Tea Room
Main Road, Farthinghoe, Northants NN13 5PB
Tel: 01295 712490
www.limesfarm.com

141 Luton Hoo
The Mansion House, Luton, Beds LU1 3TQ
Tel: 01582 734437
www.lutonhoo.co.uk

142 The Manor Buttery
Sulgrave Manor, Manor Road, Sulgrave, Northants OX17 2SD
Tel: 01295 760205
www.sulgravemanor.org.uk

143 The Mansion House
Old Warden Park, Biggleswade, Beds SG18 9DX
Tel: 01767 626200
www.themansionhouse.org

144 Mrs Dollys
34 High Street, Newport Pagnell, Bucks MK16 8AR
Tel: 07432 848227

145 The Old Tea House
7 Windsor End, Beaconsfield, Bucks HP9 2JJ
Tel: 01494 676273

146 Plantation Café
Bell Plantation, Watling Street, Towcester, Northants NN12 6GX
www.bellplantation.co.uk

147 The Rose Garden Tea Rooms
Priory House, 33 High Street South, Dunstable, Beds LU6 3RZ
Tel: 01582 890279

148 Seasons Cafe Deli
6 Market Square, Amersham, Bucks HP7 0DQ
Tel: 01494 727807

149 Sophies Tea Room at Hayden's Restaurant
The Olde Watermill, Barton Mill Lane, Barton Le Clay, Beds MK45 4RF
Tel: 01582 882672
www.haydensrestaurant.com/sophies-tea-room

150 Swanbourne Tea Rooms
26-28 Winslow Road, Swanbourne, Bucks MK17 0SW
Tel: 01296 720516

151 Teapots
31 High Street, Olney, Bucks MK46 4AA
www.teapotsolney.co.uk

152 Tea-Zels
Odell Country Park, Carlton Road, Harrold, Beds MK43 7DS
Tel: 01234 721525

153 Towcester Tea Room
169 Watling Street, Towcester, Northants NN12 6BX
Tel: 01327 358200
www.towcestertearooms.co.uk

154 Walled Garden Tea Room
Castle Ashby, Northants NN7 1LQ
Tel: 01604 695200
www.castleashbygardens.co.uk

155 Westmill Tea Room
Westmill Village Green, Nr Buntingford, Herts SG9 9LG
Tel: 01763 274236
www.westmilltearoom.co.uk

156 Woodlands Manor
Green Lane, Clapham, Beds MK41 6EP
Tel: 01234 363281
www.woodlandsmanorhotel.co.uk

THE FOODIE GUIDE AWARD WINNERS FOR 2013 . . .

These restaurants have been voted the best in each of the four counties by our readers for this year. Thank you for all your nominations and congratulations to Mrs Phillips from Hertfordshire who had her name drawn as the winner of our 2013 prize draw.

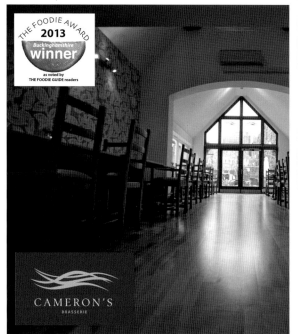

fine food and wine

The Deli Barn

Heart of the Shires
The Barn
Unit 7
A5 Watling Street
Nr Weedon
Northamptonshire
NN6 4LB
Tel: 01327 342269
Email: hicklingfinefoods@aol.co.uk
www.thedelibarn.co.uk

Opening times:
Mon-Sun 10.00 am - 5.00 pm

The Deli Barn and The Wine Barn came under new ownership in March 2013. New owners Daniel & Natasha Hickling are both passionate about supporting local producers. Having moved to the Northamptonshire area in 2008, they were hugely surprised at the quality and vast array of products to be found within the county and surrounding areas.

The Deli Barn is the perfect place to show off the gorgeous pastries, meats and sweet delights on offer in the county, as well as a selection of Dan & Tash's favourite cheeses. You will find freshly made filled croissants and bagels as well as a selection of speciality Scotch Eggs, with flavours such as chilli, black pudding and Scrumpy!

A selection of made to order gift hampers are also available from The Deli Barn, including chutney, cheeses, local beers and much more.

The new owners are very proud of the excellent award-winning wine, from local vineyards such as 'Fleur Fields' from Brixworth and 'Welland Valley' from Marston Trussell and all beers sold in The Wine Barn are from Northants microbreweries, with over 35 different beers on offer. There are often beer tasting events with local breweries onsite, when customers can learn about making beer and get a chance to speak to the brewers themselves! Dan & Tash are committed to continuing to grow their range of local beers, wines and ciders and surprise and delight customers too.

fine food and wine

2 Odells Yard
Stony Stratford
Milton Keynes
Buckinghamshire
MK11 1AQ
Tel: 01908 267373
Email: info@stony-wines.co.uk
www.stony-wines.co.uk

Opening times:
Mon 9:30 - 17:00
Tue-Sat 9:30 - 23:00

fine food and wine

Stony Wines is an independent wine merchant specialising in the finest vintages from the world's best producers, offering an alternative to the supermarket brands that have flooded the market. The shop holds over 250 varied wines and numerous specialist lagers, ales, ciders and spirits with the focus on quality. Everything in the shop has been chosen by our friendly, knowledgeable staff who will be all too pleased to provide advice and guidance. There is no pretention here, just great, interesting wines and beverages for any budget!

After having a browse, guests can treat themselves to their preferred bottle to takeaway or drink at one of our tables within the shop. A menu of light bites from our Delicatessen and Tapas Bar will be available to complement your drinks.

Venue Hire
Stony Wines is available for exclusive private hire and is an ideal location for an intimate event.

3 Odells Yard
Stony Stratford, Milton Keynes
Buckinghamshire MK11 1AQ
Tel: 01908 267373
Email: info@camerons-deli.co.uk
www.camerons-deli.co.uk

Opening times:
Mon 9:30 - 17:00
Tue-Sat 9:30 - 23:00
Tapas service times:
Tue-Sat 11:00 - 14:45 & 18:15 - 22:00
Other food is available outside of these times

CAMERON'S
TAPAS BAR AND DELICATESSEN

Following on from the success of Cameron's Brasserie, the talented team and Chef Owner Dan Cameron have opened Cameron's Delicatessen and Tapas Bar in the beautiful setting of Odell's Yard, Stony Stratford. The Cameron's ethos stays true with the emphasis on ingredients and produce of the highest quality. You'll find wonderful food with local produce featuring high on our stock list.

We stock classic deli produce and have an extensive cheese and meat counter. Many of our suppliers are small artisan producers and so you won't find most of our products in the supermarkets! Cameron's Delicatessen and Tapas Bar also provides tasty, quality ready to eat foods to eat in or takeaway. Our entire range of ready to eat food is made in-house daily, from soups to specialty sandwiches. We also have on offer cakes, pastries, and drinks such as freshly ground coffee and squeezed juices. We offer sandwiches, charcuterie, cheeses, pies and soups amongst daily specials to eat in or takeaway. In addition to these we also offer platters for sharing, choose from our suggestions or alternatively, mix and match items from our deli counter to create your own personalized platter. We serve food right through the day and you are always welcome to pop in for a bite to eat or drink.

In the evening the delicatessen is transformed into a vibey, relaxed tapas bar with the added bonus of the shop staying open! Treat yourself to some of our small plates complemented by a delicious tipple from our extensive selection. We have over 250 wines available by the bottle, craft lagers on draught, local ciders and cocktails just to name a few!

So whether you're looking for a hot drink, daily newspaper, a delicious pork pie, a bottle of wine or a superb local cider make sure you come and see us at Cameron's Delicatessen and Tapas bar soon!

fine food and wine

the larder

The Old Farmyard
Castle Ashby
Northamptonshire
NN7 1LF
Tel: 01604 696742
Email: enquiries@thelarderuk.co.uk
www.thelarderuk.co.uk

The Larder is a delicatessen located at Castle Ashby Rural Shopping Yard in the beautiful Northamptonshire countryside. With ample free parking, a selection of boutique shops to choose from and the Castle Ashby gardens to enjoy, we are well worth a visit.

Specialising in:

- Artisan Cheese
- Oils & vinegars
- Bread, cakes & biscuits
- Handmade chocolates

- Anti pasti
- Kitchen Cupboard
- Wine, beer & spirits
- Hampers

- Charcuterie
- Frozen meals
- Sweets & treats
- Kitchenware

We are proud to say that we stock over 40 carefully chosen artisan cheeses including local, British and European. We have an excellent mix of soft, medium, hard and blue cheese made with milk from cows, sheep, goats and buffalo and including pasteurised, unpasteurised, organic and cheese suitable for vegetarians.

We always have our customers' firm favourites whilst including some cheeses that are a little out of the ordinary or only available for short seasons. We all love cheese and are very happy to help you choose something that you know you will like or to challenge your tastebuds!

Our range of anti pasti includes delicious award winning Italian and Greek olives, vegetables and fruits stuffed with cream or feta cheese, balsamic onions and a mix of marinated fish.

Our British and continental hams, cured meats, salami and paté selection means you can be certain of finding something you like whilst the award winning scotch eggs and locally made, pies, pasties and quiches ensure our customers return to us time and again. Our fully personalised service means you can have as much or as little as you would like.

Our extremely popular oil and vinegar station consists of a selection of premium organic and infused olive oils as well as unusual fruit balsam vinegars - all available on tap! You can try before you buy, the team is always available to help you make the right selection and our refill service means you can bring your bottle back and try something new.

The Larder offers a vast selection of kitchen cupboard staples and delicious accompaniments. Preserves, pickles, chutneys and sauces are complemented by a carefully-selected range of dressings, mustards, dips and other delectable accompaniments. Or stock up your own larder with our wide range of cereal, porridge, pasta, biscuits, cakes, baking essentials and nibbles.

We now have a superb range of over 30 delicious Belgian chocolates which are sure to please even the most discerning palate! These luxury chocolates are suitable for any festive occasion and also make great gifts for your loved ones!

As well as international wines, the shop also sells a range of locally brewed beers, wines and spirits and is keen to promote Northamptonshire producers wherever possible.

Pick up a picnic - If you're planning a fun day out with the family, a romantic lunch on the river, or proms in the park, The Larder can pack you up a picnic chosen by you. Call in or telephone us to discuss what you would like and we will take all the hard work away from you – you can even give us your own hamper to fill if you wish!

Our bespoke hampers continue to be as popular as ever - whether it's a corporate gift or for special friends, celebrating a birthday, anniversary or Christmas, we can create the perfect hamper for you. You can either simply tell us your budget and leave the selection to us or visit the shop and personally choose the contents. Leave it with us and we will make sure it looks stunning and is beautifully gift wrapped at no extra cost. Nationwide delivery service available or you can collect.

We look forward to welcoming you to The Larder.

Opening times:
Tue-Sat 10.00 am - 5.00 pm
Sundays & Bank Holidays 11.00 am - 5.00 pm

Closed:
Christmas Day, Boxing Day & New Year's Day

fine food and wine

fine food and wine

Love Food. Love Frosts.

At Frosts we believe in providing good quality, affordable fresh food, for good living. We source only the finest ingredients and hand select all of our products to compliment seasonal changes.

We stock an extensive range of products including locally sourced fresh fruit and vegetables, hand made cakes and pies and a wide range of packaged produce from baked beans and cereals to artisan chutneys. Our fully stocked delicatessen counter offers delicious cheeses, pâtés and olives which taste fantastic alongside our bread which is baked freshly every morning. Whether you are looking for that extra treat for a dinner party or simply need a pint of milk, Frosts Food Hall offers great value convenience shopping.

Open seven days a week we have created a shopping experience that will meet all of your culinary requirements.

Woburn Country Foods Butchers Counter

Woburn Country Foods butchers counter, located in Frosts Food Hall is fully staffed and completely stocked with top quality local meats from the surrounding counties. They are committed to sourcing only the best meats from Bedfordshire and Buckinghamshire, giving customer's peace of mind that only local produce is stocked…and all at Farmers Market prices.

Frosts Garden Centre at Woburn Sands, Newport Road, Woburn Sands, Milton Keynes, MK17 8UE **Tel:** 01908 583511

www.frostsgroup.com

The Pantry
at Potterspury

Wakefield Country Courtyard
Potterspury
Northamptonshire
NN12 7QX
Tel: 01327 811511
Email: sc.01@btinternet.com
www.facebook.com/ThePantryAtPotterspury

Traditional Butcher At our Butcher's counter you will not only find top quality, locally sourced meats but also the opportunity to "chew the fat" with a real, live traditional butcher. He will be more than happy to discuss any aspects of his trade with you, including the ingredients used in handmade sausages or proper beef burgers. He can also enlighten you on the ageing and maturing of best British beef, free-range pork, succulent bacon, sweet tender lamb, free-range poultry, wild venison and game in season. We also offer a selection of freshly made home cooked meats, pies and quiches which are made each day on the premises.

Farm Shop Here, amongst other things, you will find a full range of Wessex Mill Flour (including Gluten Free) for the avid home baker. For those not given to home baking, we have a selection of bread and rolls which are baked fresh on the premises every day. We also have a selection of homemade cakes. You will also find a selection of seasonable, fresh vegetables, fruits and salad along with free-range eggs, butter and cream. Locally produced honey, jams and preserves are also stocked. Coming soon will be a selective range of fine wines and local beers.

Delicatessen At the delicatessen counter you will discover a range of gourmet foods, including chicken liver paté, goose fat (perfect for roast potatoes), Mediterranean delights such as marinated olives and antipasti dishes. The cheese counter has a range of traditional English cheese and an ever increasing selection of both English and Continental artisan hard and soft cheeses made from goat, sheep and cows milk and all from award winning producers. To complement the cheeses there is a selection of pickles and chutneys from near and far.

Outside Catering Whatever the occasion its always great to be able to rely on someone else to help with the food and drink. So when you're next planning a gathering of people, why not consider our pig roast or barbeque - we can also run an outside bar for you.

Gift Hampers We offer a personalised gift hamper service. Choose the size of hamper you would like and then fill it with your choice of products from our Pantry. Delivery can also be arranged.

Opening times:
Tue, Wed, Fri, Sat 9.00 am - 5.00 pm
Thur 9.00 am - 7.00 pm
Sun 10.00 am - 4.00 pm
Closed Mondays except Bank Holidays

fine food and wine

63 High Street
Newport Pagnell
MK16 8AT
Tel: 01908 410501
Email: eat@pic-nics.co.uk
www.pic-nics.co.uk
Facebook: www.facebook.com/PicNicsNewportPagnell
Twitter: @pic_nics

Opening times:
Mon-Fri 8.30 am - 4.00 pm
Sat 9.00 am - 4.00 pm
Sun currently closed

PicNic's arrived on the High Street of Newport Pagnell in July 2012 and is owned and run by self-confessed foodie, Nicola O'Brien.

Combining a café with a small retail area, PicNic's is a one-stop food haven.

The deli counter features an interesting collection of cheeses, olives and antipasti and cured meats as well as locally produced corned beef, pastrami and award winning pies.

The local element doesn't stop there as a further browse of the shelves will reveal jams, chutneys, condiments, oils and juices all produced in Buckinghamshire and the neighbouring counties. Being local isn't a prerequisite however as Nicola is continually sourcing and adding to the product range in a bid to find the best tasting products from artisan producers.

So if you're looking for some interesting ingredients, a foodie gift or a giant hamper packed full of tasty treats then PicNic's has it covered.

As well as selling quality ingredients, the chefs at PicNic's (they have two qualified chefs on the team!) like to use the ingredients available in the deli in their own creations. Making and baking as much as they can in house you'll find the cheeses and olives in their quiches, the chorizo in their soup and the stunning dressings and locally produced chilli sauces transforming a salad or a sandwich in to a meal to remember. It's best to get in early for lunch though – the infamous sausage rolls have been known to sell out as soon as they leave the oven!

If it's liquid refreshment you're looking for then you won't be disappointed by the selection on offer. With 100% Arabica, hand roasted Union Coffee, teapigs teas and Marimba hot chocolate (made with a whole bar of chocolate!), freshly made healthy fruit smoothies (boosted with a Matcha shot if you like!) and creamy milkshakes they're sure to have the perfect thirst quencher.

PicNic's culinary delights aren't restricted to Newport Pagnell as they now operate an outside catering service offering working lunches, buffets and canapé receptions for business meeting, parties, gatherings and events with free delivery across Milton Keynes.

fine food and wine

Browns of Stagsden
FARM SHOP

Manor Farm
High Street
Stagsden
Bedford
MK43 8SQ
Tel: 01234 822330
Email: info@brownsofstagsden.co.uk
www.brownsofstagsden.co.uk

The Brown family has farmed in and around Bedfordshire for many years, and three generations are now involved in the business. The family has always taken great pride in growing crops and rearing cattle, pigs and turkeys, so they decided to open a shop at Manor Farm, in the beautiful village of Stagsden.

Christmas Turkeys have been sold from the farm since 1949. The shop opened in 2005 and with an extension in 2008 offers a wide range of locally grown produce to an ever increasing customer base.

Traditional breeds of cattle, pigs and turkeys are reared for the shop using home-grown grain where possible, whilst lambs and free range chickens are reared locally. The beef is hung for at least three weeks for maximum tenderness and flavour.

Game is also available when in season. All sausages, burgers and ready meals are prepared on site and you will also be able to buy local vegetables, cheeses, hams, organic flour, fresh bread, gluten-free cakes, free range eggs, local milk, ice-creams and tempting accompaniments. Why not also come and try our home cured bacon and charcuterie or our home cured turkey bacon?

In the run up to Christmas - a very busy time of the year for Browns - you will be able to pre-order your home-reared turkey and any other meats, or choose from our wide range of hampers which make for excellent presents.

So if you are looking for something different and enjoy good quality produce, please pay the shop a visit, where our helpful staff will offer you a warm welcome. Why not stop and enjoy a coffee whilst you shop with us?

Opening times:
Tue-Thur 9.00 am - 5.00 pm
Fri 9.00 am - 6.00 pm
Sat 9.00 am - 4.00 pm

Follow us on Facebook and Twitter

fine food and wine

fine food and wine

BOYCOTT FARM SHOP

Welsh Lane, Stowe, Bucks MK18 5DJ
Tel: 01280 821286
Email: shop@boycottfarm.co.uk
PLEASE VISIT OUR WEBSITE FOR MORE INFORMATION AND OUR LATEST NEWS AND OFFERS
www.boycottfarm.co.uk

Boycott farm shop is situated in the middle of beautiful North Buckinghamshire countryside, close to the National Trust Estate at Stowe. Our wonderful 17c barn was sensitively restored and converted in 2008, and is now home to our popular Farm Shop, Award Winning Butchery and The Hayloft Restaurant and Tearoom.

As a working family farm we rear and produce premium quality Aberdeen Angus Beef and Traditional Breed Pork along with our fresh, free-range eggs. Using our own and local produce, we prepare a wonderful selection of homemade cakes, quiches and an extensive range of wholesome ready meals which we sell in our Farm Shop and serve in The Hayloft. Alongside our own produce our shop is well stocked with bread, milk, vegetables and much more. We also offer a Catering Selection so you can pre-order a range of foods for meetings, parties and special gatherings.

Described as an "oasis" in the Buckinghamshire countryside, The Hayloft Restaurant and Tearoom serves delicious homemade food, freshly made to order. From Monday to Friday we offer All Day Full English Breakfast, Lunch and Afternoon Tea. On Sundays, we serve Roast Sunday Lunch with hand carved meat, homemade Yorkshire puddings, roast potatoes and gravy. We offer good quality food at an honest price.

We believe in good, old fashioned customer service and are very proud of our friendly, helpful staff. You will always receive a warm welcome at Boycott Farm.

Opening times:
SHOP:
Mon-Sat 8.00 am - 6.00 pm
Sun 10.00 am - 4.00 pm

BUTCHERY:
Mon-Sat 8.00 am - 5.00 pm
Sun 10.00 am - 4.00 pm

THE HAYLOFT:
Mon-Fri 9.00 am - 5.00 pm
Sat 8.30 am - 5.00 pm
Sun 10.00 am - 4.00 pm

PERCYS
BBQ FOOD DELIVERED
MILTON KEYNES

WWW.PERCYS-DELIVERED.CO.UK

Percys
2 Darin Court
Crownhill
Milton Keynes
MK8 0AD

Call 01908 568007 to place your order

Percys has boldly challenged the takeaway market by launching a completely unique concept – BBQ FOOD DELIVERED. This is real American style smoked and slow cooked BBQ food. With authentic BBQ sauces made on the premises, a local butcher selecting unique cuts of meat, the use of real hickory smoke, dry rubs and slow cooking techniques – the menu at Percys is something you'll want to try!

With exciting cuts of meat such as hand-pulled pork shoulder and slow smoked brisket of beef, which are both packed full of flavour and melt in your mouth. Percys cut their own Slaw, which is sweetened with apple, and make their own authentic BBQ beans, mac 'n' cheese and meaty gravy, showing their passion for good tasting food and also that fast food can be real food.

Desserts aren't forgotten either with a proper New York baked vanilla cheesecake that is made in the USA and their own Sundae creations with homemade sauces.

It is simple and easy to order a Percys and you can opt to either collect or have it delivered (subject to their delivery area). There are lots of options to customise your meal and with everything freshly cooked and made to order, you can be assured of a real treat. To find out more about Percys and how you can have this food delivered to your door tonight, check out our website or give us a call.

On cup: 100% Biodegradable — Congratulations, you've used a cup...

The Bull Pen

The Bull Pen is a delightful tearoom where you will find a warm and inviting ambience amid natural oak, and timber beams.

Visit our beautiful tearoom serving exquisite cream teas, delicious homemade cakes and lunches, all in one of England's most pleasant locations.

Opening Times:
Open every day from 8.30am - 5pm (last food orders at 4.30)

The Bull Pen, embraces the unassuming natural beauty of the 220 acre farm and rural shopping village on which it resides, whilst only 16 miles from Marble Arch, it's *the* place to eat in Radlett.

Contact us now to book your table
01923 857505 | info@thebullpenrestaurant.co.uk
www.thebullpenrestaurant.co.uk

BEST BUTCHERS Ltd

Unit 5
Lower Rectory Farm
Great Brickhill
Milton Keynes
MK17 9AF
Tel: 01908 375275
Email: shop@thebestbutchers.co.uk
www.thebestbutchers.co.uk

Quality, variety and a commitment to personal service sum up Simon Boddy's "Best Butchers Ltd".

Situated on a working organic farm Best Butchers is owned and run by Simon Boddy. Since 1994 Simon has been specialising in supplying locally sourced meat and is justly proud to supply most of the best restaurants in the area.

Besides joints and fine cuts of beef, lamb, pork and poultry this absolutely spotless shop is renowned for its fine pork, beef and lamb sausages all prepared on the premises along with bacon, dry-cured and slowly smoked over beech.

Recently Simon has added a maturation room for salamis and air dried meats. The process involves patience and products are only made available when absolutely ready. Having spent a number of years developing, the team are now actively encouraging customers to compare their product against European counterparts – I think they will be pleasantly surprised. Brickhill ham is Simon's own adaption of Parma ham.

Acclaimed by Rose Prince of the Daily Telegraph that the air-dried coppa was the best air-dried meat she had tasted in Britain and the Sunday Observer rated them as "Best Deli".

Opening times:
Mon-Tue Closed
Wed 8.00 am - 12.00 pm
Thur-Fri 8.00 am - 5.00 pm
Sat 8.00 am - 2.00 pm
Sun Closed

fine food and wine

DELICATESSEN ESTRELLA

2A High Street
Winslow
Buckinghamshire
MK18 3HF
Tel: 01296 712466
www.delicatessenestrella.co.uk

Located in the heart of the pretty market town in Winslow, right opposite the Market Square, Delicatessen Estrella specialises in providing the best food and ingredients available to bring you the flavours of the Mediterranean. Helen and John Knight have a passion for all food, especially that of Spain and North Africa and always stock an excellent range of unusual Spanish products, including charcuterie and cheeses.

Throughout the shop the emphasis is always on food of the highest quality, which they source from the best suppliers in their fields, including cheeses from Neal's Yard Dairy and Spanish meats from Brindisa. Helen's home cooking is a huge hit with customers. From home baked pasties, pies, quiches and cakes through to a seasonally changing selection of delicious

homemade, ready prepared, frozen bistro meals and accompaniments, all using local meat and produce. In summer, fresh salads are available and in the colder months, seasonal soups to take home. An excellent range of ethically produced coffees are ground to order and fresh artisan bread is available several days a week.

Estrella opens every Friday night until 7pm to make it easy for busy workers to pick up a one stop meal. This might range from a tapas selection or an antipasto plate to a cheese board, cake or pudding. Complement your food with their selection of great wines and sherries, or try a few bottles from a popular range of locally brewed real ales.

So if you love good food and are looking for the best products and ingredients for yourself, or a food or drink related gift like their popular Christmas baskets and hampers made to order, make sure you visit Delicatessen Estrella.

Opening times:
Mon-Thur 10:00 – 17:30
Fri 10:00 – 19:00
Sat 09:30 – 17:00
Sun Farmers Market Sundays (1st Sunday of each month) and December 10:00 – 14:00

V

fine food and wine

Smiths Farm Shop

fine food and wine

Chapel Brampton Shop Tel: 01604 843206
Brampton Lane, Chapel Brampton, Northampton, Northants NN6 8AA
Mon-Sat 9.00am - 5.30pm Sun 10.00am - 1.00pm
Email: smithsfarmshop@btinternet.com **www.smithsfarmshop.co.uk**

Now at three convenient locations within Northamptonshire Smith's Farm Shop is a retailer of quality fresh farm foods and fine country produce. Selling fresh seasonal fruit and vegetables from British growers, including produce grown on their own farm situated behind the shop at Chapel Brampton. Aiming to source from producers most local ensures products arrive on the shelves in near-perfect condition, bursting with flavour and with the highest nutritional value. Regular customers say they come back time and again because Smith's produce can't be beaten for freshness and flavour, all at prices that compare well against larger U.K. food retailers.

Outside each shop you will find garden and pet supplies, plants and solid fuels. Inside the shops you will be greeted by a spacious layout for all the main food categories such as fruit and vegetables, jams and preserves, frozen foods, delicatessen, dairy products, eggs, cakes and pastries, bakery and meat. The quiet, relaxed atmosphere will help make your shopping trip more of a pleasurable experience, and less of a chore. They also stock ranges of non-food products, mainly for the home, garden and pets along with a small selection of greeting cards.

A great shopping experience awaits you at Smith's Farm Shop. For your convenience, they have a large car park right outside the shop entrances. Friendly members of staff are always ready to help carry your purchases to the car. They provide a relaxed and enjoyable shopping experience and at the Chapel Brampton site, you will find several other attractions to add a bit of fun and interest to your shopping trip!

Towcester Shop Tel: 01327 358358
Bell Plantation, Watling Street, Towcester, Northants NN12 6GX
Mon-Sun 10.00am - 4.30pm

Great Billing Shop Tel: 01604 412111
Billing Garden Village, The Causeway, Great Billing, Northants NN3 9EX
Mon-Sun 10.00am - 4.30pm

Aubergine Fine Food & Wines

73 High Street
Woburn Sands
Bucks MK17 8QY
Tel: 01908 582020
Email: auberginedeli@btconnect.com

Aubergine Fine Foods is an independent, family-owned delicatessen and wine merchant in Woburn Sands, established by local residents Jill and John Goulding. Run by food lovers for food lovers, Aubergine strives to offer international speciality foods alongside the finest locally-sourced produce. John is also happy to share his expert advice to help find a perfect wine match for any food.

The ever expanding range includes British and continental cheeses, salamis and chorizos, pastas, cooking sauces, preserves, chocolates, breads and biscuits, plus all the kitchen cupboard essentials.

Wherever possible Aubergine sources foods from local, small-scale producers, including free-range eggs from Lidlington; bacon, sausages and hams from their butcher's own farm in Bedfordshire; bread from Ampthill; plus

Opening times:
Mon-Fri 8.00 am - 5.00 pm
Sat 9.00 am - 4.00 pm

honey, vegetables and delicious home-made cakes from Woburn Sands itself.

In addition, there is an increasing range of 'free from' foods for people with special dietary requirements, including gluten-free pastas, cereals and biscuits. Aubergine is also an ethical and environmentally responsible business. Many products are fairly traded, offering producers in the developing world a better deal, and all the shop's own packaging is bio-degradable, recyclable, or from a sustainable source.

Latest developments include a new lunch menu offering pasta dishes, home-made savoury tartlets, filled ciabatta rolls and gourmet salads, plus great coffee and fresh fruit smoothies. A business and event menu is also available with free local delivery. And for those of you looking for something a bit different for your special event or even wedding, we can provide a portable wood fired pizza oven with your personal pizza chef.

Whatever your culinary tastes, if you're passionate about food and looking for an alternative to the supermarket experience, pay a visit to Aubergine - your local, independent fine food store.

fine food and wine

SUMMERHILL FARM SHOP

Cople Road, Cardington, Bedfordshire MK44 3SH
Tel: 01234 831222
Email: sales@summerhillfarmshop.co.uk
www.summerhillfarmshop.co.uk

Set in the picturesque village of Cardington, home of the famous Cardington airship hangars, Summerhill Farm Shop takes great pride in sourcing the very best in local and seasonal produce. The shop is now under the management of Sarah Fuller and new Head Butcher James Fraser.

We are part of the Southill Estate which raises entirely grass-fed British White cattle for sale exclusively through the farm shop. The beef is hung for the full, traditional 28 days, allowing it to mature on the bone for that unique flavour and tenderness that can only be achieved by the maturing process. Cuts and joints can be ordered in advance and viewed over time whilst they are maturing. Such is the demand for our White beef that we do need to source some additional local beef but always ensure that it is farmed ethically and in line with our own very high standards of husbandry. Our lamb and freerange chicken are sourced from farms within Cardington village and the pork is from nearby St Neots. All of our meat is expertly butchered on site to the customers' exact requirements but, in addition to the more traditional cuts, handmade sausages and burgers, there is an extensive range of our own gourmet and "ready to cook" lines such as chicken filo pastries, stir fries, marinated meats and the Summerhill Traditional Pork Sausage, winner of Bedford's Best Sausage (Taste Real Food – Bedford). And of course we have local turkeys for Christmas!

The Southill Estate is also home to Warden Abbey Vineyard, Bedfordshire's only working vineyard, and their range of English wine including the award-winning Warden Abbot Sparkling is available in the farm shop along with a bespoke selection of South African and new world wines sourced by Charles Whitbread, owner of the Estate. We also stock a wide range of English fruit and country wines and several locally produced beers, ales and ciders.

Our deli counter has a great range of carefully selected artisan and award-winning cheeses, mainly from within the UK, and cold meats including the delicious Bedfordshire Black Ham, Suffolk salami and chorizo, olives and antipasti, pies, quiches and patés. The cheese and meat are complemented by a very good choice of savoury biscuits and chutneys and pickles all sourced as locally as possible. Other local produce includes eggs which are all free-range from the same farm in Cardington as our chickens, cakes, fruit pies and bread produced by local bakers and delivered daily. In addition, we work very closely with local farmers' co-operatives and distributors to source local fruit and vegetables, grown naturally and in season.

Opening times:
Mon-Fri 9.00 am - 6.00 pm
Sat 8.00 am - 5.00 pm
Sun 10.00 am - 4.00 pm

We can be found just three miles south east of Bedford – exit from the A421 at the Sandy A603 junction and follow the signs to Summerhill Farm Shop and Cardington from the roundabout.

Pecks FARM SHOP

Stockwell Farm
Eggington
Leighton Buzzard
Bedfordshire LU7 9PA
Shop: 01525 211859
Office: 01525 210281
www.pecksfarmshop.co.uk

Pecks Farm Shop is a small family run business based in Eggington on the outskirts of Leighton Buzzard in Bedfordshire.

Our shop which was opened in October 2002 presents a wonderful mouthwatering feast of high quality country cuisine, much of it fresh and locally produced.

We have been farming here for over fifty years as a dairy farm with our own dairy; Eggington Dairy, which to this day still delivers to homes and businesses in the area.

As a farming family we care passionately about our food; where it comes from, how it has been grown. Our product focus is on quality and that it is local and most importantly, fresh.

We offer a wide selection of fruit and vegetables as well as cheeses from around the country with many coming from specialist firms. Home prepared meals, milk, eggs, butter, yogurt, cream, fresh bread, sausage rolls, Cornish pasties and locally renowned "Bunkers sausages" are just some of the delicious goods we have in our shop.

We also offer a superb range of specialist products like black pudding and black bacon from Woburn Country Foods together with a selection of handmade mustards, pickles and chutneys, the ideal accompaniment.

We are the local stockists of Lime Tree Pantry Pies, one of the country's premier suppliers.

We have a large selection of award winning English wines from Bedfordshire, Cambridgeshire and Oxfordshire and the best selection of bottled real ales in the county!

Our stunning hampers, beautifully wrapped can be delivered anywhere in the UK.

Opening times:
Mon-Wed 9.00 am - 6.00 pm
Thur 9.00 am - 7.30 pm
Fri 9.00 am - 6.00 pm
Sat 9.00 am - 5.00 pm
Sun 10.00 am - 3.00 pm

fine food and wine

FARMERS MARKETS

Whilst every effort has been made compiling this list, we cannot accept responsibility when dates/times/places are changed.

Bedfordshire

Ampthill	The Prince of Wales pub car park	Last Saturday every month (except December)	9.00am - 1.00pm
Bedford	Harpur Square	2nd & 4th Thursday every month	9.00am - 2.00pm
Biggleswade	Market Square	3rd Wednesday every month	9.00am - 2.00pm
Cranfield	The Cross Keys pub	2nd Sunday every month	9.00am - 1.00pm
Dunstable Downs	Chiltern Gateway Centre	1st Sunday every month (except January)	10.00am - 2.00pm
Leighton Buzzard	High Street	3rd Saturday every month	9.00am - 2.00pm
Milton Ernest	Garden Centre Country Food Fayre	3rd Saturday every month	10.00am - 3.00pm
Sandy	Sandy Car Park	1st Saturday every month (except January)	9.00am - 1.00pm
Shefford	High Street	2nd Saturday every month	9.00am - 1.00pm
Woburn	The Pitching's, Woburn	3rd Sunday every month	11.00am - 3.00pm

Buckinghamshire

Aylesbury	Old Market Square	4th Tuesday every month	9.00am - 2.00pm
Beaconsfield	Windsor End, The Old Town	4th Saturday every month	9.00am - 12.30pm
Buckingham	Old Cattle Pens, High Street	1st Tuesday every month	7.30am - 1.00pm
Little Chalfont	Village Hall car park, Cokes Lane	2nd Saturday every month	9.00am - 1.00pm
Marlow	Dean Street car park	Every Sunday	10.00am - 1.00pm
Newport Pagnell	Market Hill, High Street	3rd Friday every month	9.00am - 2.00pm
Olney	Market Place	1st Sunday every month	10.00am - 2.00pm
Prestwood	Hildreths Garden Centre, Wycombe Rd.	Every Friday	8.00am - 1.00pm
Princes Risborough	High Street	3rd Thursday every month	8.30am - 1.30pm
Stony Stratford	Market Square	Last Friday every month	8.30am - 1.30pm
Wendover	Off High Street	3rd Saturday every month	10.00am - 1.00pm
Winslow	Market Square	First Sunday every month	11.00am - 2.00pm
Wolverton	Market Halls car park, Town Hall	1st & 3rd Saturdays every month	9.00am - 1.00pm

Hertfordshire

Dane End	Dane End Memorial Hall	2nd Saturday every month	10.30am - 12.30pm
Great Amwell	Van Hage Garden Company	1st Thursday every month	9.00am - 1.00pm
Gt Hormead	Village Hall	1st Saturday every month	10.00am - 12.30pm
Harpenden	Lower High Street	4th Saturday every month	10.00am - 2.00pm
Hatfield	White Lion Square	1st Saturday every month (except January)	9.00am - 2.00pm
Hertford	Market Place	2nd Saturday every month	9.00am - 1.00pm
Hertford Heath	Village Hall	3rd Sunday every month	9.00am - 1.00pm
Hitchin	Riverside	Last Saturday every month	8.00am - 2.00pm
Hoddesdon	The Clock Tower	3rd Friday every month	9.00am - 2.00pm
Leominster	Corn Square	2nd Saturday every month	9.00am - 1.00pm
Little Hadham	Village Hall	Last Saturday every month	9.00am - 12.00pm
Royston	Town Hall	1st Friday every month	9.30am - 1.00pm
Sandon	Village Hall	3rd Saturday every month	9.30am - 12.00pm
St Albans	Town Hall	2nd Sunday every month	9.00am - 2.00pm
Tring	Market Place	Alternate Saturdays	9.00am - 12.15pm

Northamptonshire

Brackley	Market Place	3rd Saturday every month	9.00am - 1.00pm
Daventry	High Street	1st Saturday every month	8.30am - 1.30pm
Higham Ferrers	Market Square	Last Saturday every month	8.00am - 3.00pm
Kettering	Wicksteed Park	3rd Sunday every month	9.00am - 2.00pm
Northampton	Market Square	3rd Thursday every month	9.00am - 1.30pm
Oundle	Market Street	2nd Saturday every month	9.00am - 2.00pm
Towcester	Richmond Rd car park	2nd Friday every month	9.00am - 2.00pm
Wellingborough	Market Place	Last Thursday every month	9.00am - 2.00pm

Chef Profile

Murrays at Whittlebury Hall

Cooking style
Modern seasonal British with international and classical influences.

Current speciality
The dish I'm most proud of on the menu currently is the Guinea Fowl with truffles, figs, pancetta and lemon – the different textures, combinations with flavours and visual theatre on the plate.

Training or background
I have spent over 14 years working in various hotels and restaurants in the UK and overseas, previously at Fawsley Hall Hotel, 3 AA rosettes, and before that at the Dormy House Hotel in Broadway, 2 AA rosettes, as well as Brocket Hall.

What cookbooks would you recommend?
The French Laundry by Thomas Keller, he has a reputation for his culinary skills and high standards, and for being the only American chef to hold multiple three star Michelin ratings, and Alinea by Grant Achatz.

When travelling abroad or on holiday, what food do you most enjoy?
Whether on holiday in the UK or abroad, a big bowl of Mussels Mariniere with fresh crusty bread is just perfect!

How do you keep up with the latest cooking innovations?
Innovation can be drawn from the many celebrated chefs out there. One of the chefs I admire the most is John Campbell, one of the UK's most talented chefs with a reputation for innovation, expertise and achieving two Michelin stars.

What kitchen tool couldn't you live without?
My set of knives – they really have worked hard over the years!

Damyan Stefanov

In The Kitchen

Cotswold White Chicken with Stuffing, Pancetta, Apricots, Young Leeks and Girolles

Ingredients - Serves 4

- 4 Cotswold Chicken Breasts

Chicken jus:
- 5kg Chicken Wings
- 500g Miropiox of Veg
  (carrot leeks onion celery)
- 20g Fresh Herbs

Stuffing:
- 50g Pancetta
- 50g Shallot

- 50g Breadcrumbs
- 5g Chopped Chervil
- 50g Hot Chicken Stock
- 10g Butter

Cep soil (dirty potatoes):
- 100g Jersey Royal Potatoes
- 15g Flour
- 5g Ground Almonds
- 7.5g Butter

- 1g Salt
- 1g Cocoa powder
- 1g Cep powder

Apricot puree:
- 100g Dried Apricot
- 50g White Wine
- 50g Stock Syrup
  (equal sugar and water)

For garnish: 12 Baby Leeks

Method

For the Chicken: Trim the excess sinew from the breast then season the chicken with salt and pepper in a tray with oil. Place a pan on the stove to heat. Once the pan is hot place the seasoned chicken skin side down into the pan, then place the pan in a pre-heated oven at 200°c for 8 minutes. Then turn the chicken and leave in the oven for a further 4 minutes and then leave to rest on the cooling rack.

For the Chicken Jus: Place half the chicken wings on the tray and cook at 180°c for 30 minutes (or until golden brown), then add the prepped miropiox of vegetable to the hot saucepan and cook for a further 30 minutes. Once complete add the chicken wings, cover with water and simmer for 12 hours, remembering to skim off the fat. Then roast the remainder of the wings at 180°c for 1 hour. Strain the stock into another pan and add the freshly roasted bones and simmer for a further 12 hours. Once simmering is completed strain the stock and skim. Then start reducing the stock until sauce consistency. Add fresh herbs and infuse for 2 minutes, then place through muslin.

For the Shallot & Pancetta Stuffing: Brunoix the shallot and pancetta and sweat them with no colour in separate pans. Add 5g of butter to each pan and wait until it starts to foam. Then combine all the ingredients into a bowl and mix together. Place the mixture onto greaseproof paper and roll flat with a thickness of 2mm. Cut into rectangle shape pieces. To reheat the stuffing, place it in the oven for 30 seconds.

For the Dirty Potatoes: Place the Jersey Royal potatoes into water and wash thoroughly. Then bring to boil in salted water and simmer for 10 minutes (or until cooked). Allow to cool then peel the skin being careful not to damage the potatoes. To make the soil, combine all ingredients together until it turns into a crumb consistency, then place in a pre-heated oven at 180°c for 6 minutes. Allow to cool and pass through a fine sieve. Finally re-heat the potatoes in boiling water for 30 seconds and toss in butter, season and sprinkle the soil over the potatoes.

For the Apricot Purée:
Place all the ingredients in a tub and leave for 24 hours, then blitz and pass through a fine sieve.

Chef Profile

Cooking style
Modern English and a few of the classical dishes.

Current speciality
Aylesbury Duckling cooked traditionally and our new tasting menu.

Training or background
Trainee chef at the King's Head, Ivinghoe; Grosvenor House, Park Lane; Randolph Hotel, Oxford; Senior Sous Chef, Pendley Manor Hotel, Tring; Le Belle Epoque, South Kensington, Sous Chef; Brocket Hall, Hertfordshire, Head Chef; Auberge du Lac, Hertfordshire, Senior Sous Chef and back to the King's Head, Ivinghoe as Head Chef and one of the three owners.

What do you love most about your job?
The service – seeing the food go out to the guests as perfect as possible (and seeing the empty plates come back!)

What prompted you to become a Chef?
My father, who was a great chef and inspiration.

Which seasonal produce do you look forward to?
English asparagus, peas and berries.

How do you like to unwind?
Spending time with my 2 children, eating and drinking, going to the gym.

What's your preferred home cooked meal?
Christmas dinner cooked by my mother.

The Kings Head, Ivinghoe

Jonathan O'Keeffe

In The Kitchen

Ingredients

- Zest and Juice of 2 ½ Lemons
- 4 Whole Eggs
- 1 Egg Yolk
- 175g Sugar

For the pastry:
- 250g Flour
- 125g Butter at room temperature
- 65g Icing Sugar
- 2 Egg Yolks
- 1/2 tbsp Double Cream

Method

1 *For the pastry:* Beat the butter and icing sugar until smooth.
2 Beat in the egg yolks, then flour and double cream until a pastry is formed.
3 Knead into a ball, cover with cling film and place in fridge for 1 hour to rest.
4 Roll pastry on a floured surface to form a 12" circle.
5 Line a buttered 8" tart ring with the pastry and trim off edges. Bake blind for 25 mins at 350ºF, then remove baking beans and cook for a further 5 mins.
6 *For the lemon filling:* Whisk the eggs, egg yolk, sugar, cream, juice and zest of lemons until smooth and strain through a sieve.
7 Pour the mixture into the tart mould and bake for 30 mins at 175ºF.
8 Check often towards the end of cooking time – the tart should have a little "wobble" in the middle.
9 Cool for 1 hour and serve with whipped cream and seasonal berries.

Lemon Tart

Chef Profile

St Helena Restaurant

Cooking style
Modern with a mix of classic methods with big attention to purity of flavour!!!

Current speciality
Duck with Smoked Eel and Pineapple or a Lamb Loin and Braised Neck with Peas, Broad Beans, Garlic and Sea Aster, simple but stunning.

Training or background
Trained at Flitwick Manor for 4 years under Richard Walker then Rushton Hall in Northamptonshire and 3 years in Devon.

What new ingredients or techniques have you found useful recently?
I think techniques are changing, an "old fashioned" way of cooking is coming back, instead of doing hot jellys and foams it's all about flavour now, to get the best out of it, I like a little bit of foraged only if it tastes good, not just to be fashionable.

When travelling abroad or on holiday, what food do you most enjoy?
I love staying in the UK to eat, I think we have some of the best restaurants and chefs in the world. I just love Michael Wignall, Daniel Clifford and Tom Aikens food, simply amazing iconic figures of our industry.

What country do you think has the best food?
Spain and England.

What technique is simple but impressive?
Sous Vide cooking, you can cook a bit of pork belly on 75°c for 12 hours and it comes out just amazing, pure porky flavour.

What's been your biggest disaster in the kitchen?
One place we didn't have any gas. For lunch we had 30 booked, it came back on as the guests were walking through the front door, it was a bit frantic for a few hours.

Steve Barringer

In The Kitchen

Scallop, Sweetcorn, Crispy Chicken Skin & Basil

Ingredients - Serves 4

- 12 Scallops (or 8 large)
- 500g Fresh Sweetcorn
- 800ml Milk
- 1 Gelatine Leaf
- 8g Agar Agar
- 2 Whole Fresh Corn on the Cob
- 4 Pieces of Chicken Skin
- 2 Chillis
- 1 Banana Shallot
- 10ml White Wine Vinegar
- 50ml Olive Oil
- Juice of half a Lime
- 50ml Plain Flour
- Sparkling Water
- Half a Cucumber
- Fresh Basil or Micro Basil Cress for garnish

Oven:180°c Fryer:170°c

Method

1 Sweetcorn Mousse: Cook the sweetcorn out in the milk until soft, blend in a blender until smooth, pass through a sieve, place back in the pan and add the Agar Agar until it reaches around 86°c. Take off and place on a tray in the fridge to set. Once set, place in a mixer and whisk until light and fluffy. Place in a piping bag until plating up. **2 Sweetcorn Fritter:** Take one sweetcorn, remove from cob, add to a bowl with 1 finely chopped chilli ,half a finely chopped shallot and 4 chopped basil leaves. Add the flour and salt and mix in the sparkling water until a thick batter texture and then fry in a fryer at 170°c until golden brown (around 3 minutes) then place on a paper towel to drain. **3 Sweetcorn Salsa:** Roast one sweetcorn in a pan until golden and roasted, allow to cool then remove corns from the cob and place in a bowl with half a diced shallot, a diced red chilli and half a cucumber, which has been peeled, seeds removed and thinly chopped into nice dice. Add the vinegar, olive oil and juice of half a lime to taste, then add finely chopped basil. **4** Place chicken skin on a cooling rack on a tray, season with sea salt then place in the oven for around 8-10 minutes until golden and crispy. **5** Cook the scallops, get the pan nice and hot, place them in the pan and cook until golden (takes around a minute) then add a knob of butter and turn and cook for a further one minute. Take off the heat, make sure they have a little give but not soft and not firm, then plate up with the other ingredients!!

Chef Profile

Cooking style
British with Mediterranean/European undertones and Pacific Rim.

Training or background
4 years training, Day release to Hull College of Further Education, Manor House Restaurant, Devonshire Home, Private and Corporate Hotels, Cruise Ships.

How do you cope with the long working day?
I try to take at least 1 - 1½ hr break mid afternoon.

What cookbooks would you recommend?
"The Cookery Year" and "The Book of Ingredients".

When travelling abroad or on holiday, what food do you most enjoy?
Anything local to the area, with simple ingredients is often the best.

How do you keep up with the latest cooking innovations?
TV cooking programmes and trade magazines, e.g. 'Cater' and keeping an eye on everybody else.

What kitchen tool couldn't you live without?
Carving fork or Palette knife.

What technique is simple but impressive?
Sugar work for desserts, i.e. run-outs or spun.

What's been your biggest disaster in the kitchen?
When I had only just started as a Commis Chef in 1983 I washed out a stock pot which I thought was full of dirty water but found out it was stock! (Not very good stock anyway as it was cloudy).

The Betsey Wynne

Chris Fielding

In The Kitchen

Ingredients - Serves 6
- 900ml Double Cream
- 225-250g Caster Sugar
- Juice of 3 Lemons
- 6 Wine Glasses

Method
1 Bring the cream and sugar to the boil and simmer for 2-3 minutes.
2 Add the lemon juice and mix well.
3 Remove from the heat and leave to cool slightly.
4 Pass and pour into glasses (leaving a 1cm space at the top of each glass.)
5 Refrigerate for 2-3 hours.
To serve: Pour a little double cream on top of each Posset, garnish with some fresh mint and spun sugar.

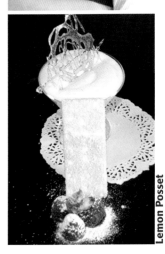
Lemon Posset

The Old Thatched Inn

Stir Fried Monkfish, Peppers & Pak Choi

Chef Profile

Cooking style
Modern British.

Current speciality
Slow cooked pork belly, it is such a versatile dish.

Training or background
I started working as a kitchen porter straight after school. In 2001 started taking a real interest in food, worked at Le Manoir Aux Quat Saisons for two years and then went on to work for John Burton-Race and Jean Christophe Novelli.

What do you love most about your job?
I have the freedom to write my own menus.

Which seasonal produce do you look forward to?
Summer Berries.

What's your favourite food combo?
Meat and fish i.e. Pork Belly and Scallops.

How do you like to unwind?
I love taking my dog on long walks and spending time with my wife.

What's your preferred home cooked meal?
My wife's Spaghetti Bolognese.

Do you have a favourite cook book?
"White Heat", Marco Pierre White.

Stuart James

In The Kitchen

Ingredients - Serves 4
- 2 x 250g Monkfish Tails (filleted)
- 2 tbsp Groundnut Oil
- 1 small Red Pepper (thinly sliced)
- 1 small Yellow Pepper (thinly sliced)
- 1 small Shallot (thinly sliced)
- 1 tbsp Chopped Ginger
- 1 small Courgette (sliced)
- 120g Pak Choi (shredded)
- 50g Fresh Beansprouts
- 2 tbsp Light Soy Sauce
- 1½tsp Chilli
- 1 tsp Sesame Oil
- Salt & Pepper to taste
- Lemon Vinaigrette

Method
1 Remove any grey membrane from the Monkfish and cut into 1½" slices.
2 Prepare all other ingredients before you start cooking.
3 Heat a large wok until almost smoking. Add one tablespoon of the oil and stir-fry the Monkfish for about three minutes until browned on both sides. Remove and drain on paper towels and keep warm.
4 Add the remaining oil, reheat, stir-fry the peppers, onion, ginger and courgette for two minutes until coloured lightly. Remove from the wok with a draining spoon and keep warm.
5 Reheat the wok and stir-fry the pak choi and beansprouts for two minutes then add the chilli. Return the other vegetables to the wok, toss in the sesame oil and reheat until very hot. Season with salt and pepper.
6 Divide among four warmed plates and arrange the Monkfish on top, trickle a little lemon vinaigrette on the top of each portion, then serve.

Chef Profile

Cooking style
French with a British and Italian influence.

Current speciality
Venison, as we are so close to Woburn Estate, we're granted with an amazing supply of great quality Venison.

Training or background
French trained, Michelin star.

How do you cope with the long working day?
By doing my paperwork, it gives me 10 minutes to sit down, stress free...most of the time!

What new ingredients or techniques have you found useful recently?
Using the Thermodyne for slow-cooking, after a demonstration with Alyn Williams at The Westbury Hotel in London.

When travelling abroad or on holiday, what food do you most enjoy?
Home cooked food by my Mum or Dad in France.

What country do you think has the best food?
France of course!

How do you keep up with the latest cooking innovations?
sharing ideas and discussing with fellow chefs.

What kitchen tool couldn't you live without?
My Thermodyne, it helps me throughout service to deliver high quantity and quality food rapidly, but it's also amazing for crisps, confit and other forms of slow cooking.

What technique is simple but impressive?
Chopping and dicing - people still marvel at the speed and accuracy a chef can do it without chopping off a finger.

What's been your biggest disaster in the kitchen?
As if I will tell you!

Ben Hars

The Swan Inn, Milton Keynes Village

In The Kitchen

Ingredients - Serves 8
- 300g Pitted Dates
- 430g Water
- 1 tbsp Golden Syrup
- 1 tbsp Black Treacle
- 1 tsp Bicarbonate of Soda
- 230g Demerara Sugar
- 85g Butter
- 3 Eggs
- 250g Self Raising Flour

Method
1 Pre-heat the oven to 160°c. Line a tray (approx. 8 by 8 inch) with baking paper.
2 In a pan, put the dates, water, syrup, treacle and bicarbonate of soda and bring to the boil for 2 minutes. Blitz down with hand blender and reserve.
3 Mix the soft butter and the sugar together, add the eggs one by one and then fold in the self raising flour.
4 Add in the date mix.
5 Pour the mix into the tray and bake in the oven for 35-45 minutes. Check with a knife, the blade should come out hot and almost clean.
6 Transfer on to a cooling rack and leave for one hour.
7 Serve warm or hot with toffee sauce and vanilla ice cream.

Sticky Toffee Pudding

The Three Tuns

Chef Profile

Cooking style
Modern English cuisine with a slight hint of French.

Current speciality
Roast Cod With a Wild Garlic Crust, Langoustine Bisque, Pearl Barley, Spinach and Pea Fricasee.

Training or background
4 years under Peter Chandler at "Paris House", 3 years at Jean Christophe-Novelli's "White Horse" at Harpenden and "French Horn" at Steppingley, eventually as his Head Chef. Then on to "The Plough" at Wavendon as Head Chef, where I gained 2 Rosettes.

How do you cope with the long working day?
Red Bull, coffee and a sandwich!

What country do you think has the best food?
The French followed closely by the Spanish.

How do you keep up with the latest cooking innovations?
Research and development, read books, experiment!

What technique is simple but impressive?
Slow Cooking, we salt our pork belly for 12 hours then cook at 86°c overnight and it is so tender.

What's been your biggest disaster in the kitchen?
Sending out a party of 40 people soufflés at Paris House, then eating a spare soufflé....then finding out it wasn't spare!

Chris Smith

In The Kitchen

Ingredients

For Sweet Pastry:
- 140g Butter
- 90g Caster Sugar
- 1 Egg
- 270g Plain Flour

For Treacle Mix:
- 300g Breadcrumbs
- 700g Golden Syrup
- 1 Lemon (Zest and Juice)
- 175ml Orange Juice
- 1 Pint Double Cream
- 3 Eggs

For Hazelnut Praline:
- 100g Hazelnuts
- 200g Caster Sugar

Method

For Sweet Pastry:
1 Cream the butter and sugar together. **2** Add egg and sieve in flour. **3** Rest for 2 hours. **4** Roll out on a surface to about a ¼ of an inch thickness. **5** Place into tart case. **6** Leave pastry overhanging around the edge as it will shrink. **7** Blind bake at 150°c for about 15 minutes.

For Treacle Mix:
1 Heat up syrup, orange juice, lemon juice. **2** Pull off heat and whisk in breadcrumbs and eggs. **3** Fold in cream. **4** Pour mixture into tart case. **5** Bake at 160°c for about 30 minutes or until mixture is set with a slight wobble.

For Hazelnut Praline:
1 Roast and peel hazelnuts (or buy them peeled and just roast). **2** Make a dry caramel by heating just caster sugar in a pan and shaking until it forms a light coloured caramel. **3** Pour over the nuts and wait for it to cool. **4** Crush with a rolling pin or in a blender. Serve with a spoon of clotted cream!

Treacle Tart

Chef Profile

Cooking style
Modern English.

Current speciality
Braised Beef Cheeks with Beetroot and Blue Cheese Risotto.

What cookbooks would you recommend?
Nico Ladenis, Walnut Tree by Franco Taruschio and any David Thompson books.

When travelling abroad or on holiday, what food do you most enjoy?
I always enjoy any local or traditional food and make a special effort to find this when I am away.

What country do you think has the best food?
Thailand.

How do you keep up with the latest cooking innovations?
Internet, TV and sampling.

What kitchen tool couldn't you live without?
Mandolin.

What technique is simple but impressive?
Risotto making.

The Old Crown

Ian Street _____

In The Kitchen

Ingredients
- 12 Quails Eggs
- 1 kg Quality Sausage Meat
- Pinch Nutmeg
- ½ tsp Celery Salt
- Pinch of Chopped Thyme
- 2 Eggs
- 300ml Milk
- 500g Fresh Breadcrumbs
- Flour for dusting

Method
1 Place quail eggs in boiling water for 4 minutes.
2 Drain eggs and place in ice water to arrest the cooking process, then peel the eggs.
3 Mix the sausage meat, nutmeg, celery salt and thyme well together.
4 Carefully mould the sausage meat mix around the cooked eggs aiming for a 1cm thick coverage.
5 Beat eggs together with the milk.
6 Dust the balls with flour.
7 Immerse the balls in egg wash lift them out slowly as to allow excess egg wash to drip off, roll the balls in the breadcrumbs, dip back in egg wash and re-roll in the breadcrumbs to coat them twice. Your eggs should be a bit bigger than a golf ball.
8 Deep fry at 160°c for 5 minutes.
9 Serve with garlic mayonnaise or a spicy tomato ketchup.

Mini Scotch Eggs

Chef Profile

Cooking style
A mixture of classic British and French with a twist.

Current speciality
Our Pan Fried Scallops with Sashimi Tuna Ceviche, with Avocado Mousse and Rocket Salad is proving very popular.

Training or background
I originally trained and worked in France. I celebrate 20 years of working in England this year, having worked in a number of country house hotels before joining Woburn, where I live on the estate with my wife Samantha and daughters Isabella and Sophia.

What new ingredients or techniques have you found useful recently?
I have recently been on a course for 'water bath'. It's amazing how tender food is when cooked this way and eggs are unbelievable.

What cookbooks would you recommend?
I enjoy Rick Stein, Jamie Oliver and Paul Hollywood as our two daughters are always wanting to try something new and are real junior foodies!

What country do you think has the best food?
As a Frenchman, I would have to say my adopted country England is a favourite. However, Italy really does have the wine, food and of course the weather.

What kitchen tool couldn't you live without?
A sharp knife every time. It's a really critical part of food preparation and I regularly sharpen mine.

What technique is simple but impressive?
Sugar work is not as difficult as people imagine, but it really does have a wow factor.

Olivier Bertho

In The Kitchen

Ingredients
- 10oz Raisins
- 8oz Sultanas
- 8oz Currants
- 4 tbsp Sherry
- 4 tbsp Port
- 4 tbsp Brandy
- 8oz Butter
- 2 tsp Mixed Spice
- 8oz Soft Brown Sugar
- 2 tbsp Black Treacle
- 4 Eggs
- 10oz Plain Flour
- Level tsp Bicarbonate of Soda
- Half tsp Salt
- 4 oz Glace Cherries
- 4 oz Candied Peel
- 2 oz Blanched Almonds

Method
1. Soak all fruit in alcohol for 24 hours.
2. Cream the butter, sugar and treacle together.
3. Add the eggs, then add flour with bicarbonate and salt in gradually.
4. Then add the marinated fruit and chopped almonds and mix well.
5. Line an 11inch baking tin with greaseproof paper and pour mixture in.
6. Bake for two and half hours at 160ºc.

Chef Profile

Cooking style
I like to think my style is modern with classic methods being used. I try not to over complicate and am very keen on seasonal and freshness of the produce.

Training or background
I started in hotels for the first 6 years, learning many different areas of the kitchen. I travelled to France for a ski season and to Dubai for the international air show. Once I returned back to the UK, I became an agency chef, learning many skills and methods. Within the last few years I have worked within restaurants, which is where I decided my future in catering will be.

What cookbooks would you recommend?
I have so many cookbooks and read them to get new ideas as well as trying the recipes. I think 'Larousse' is a must for chefs as well as the 'Flavour Thesaurus'. I'm a big fan of Michel Roux, Escoffier, Tom Kitchen, Thomas Keller, Rick Stein, Raymond Blanc & Marcus Wareing; all with their own style of cooking.

What country do you think has the best food?
For me, even being half English/Italian, the best food is French. It's where it all started with flavours and different cooking methods. Learning French ways and styles can then be used in so many dishes. Italian comes very close. I go to Italy a lot and the food down south is some of the best I've eaten. It's all about the freshness and it so works.

What kitchen tool couldn't you live without?
I'd have to say a food probe. From roasting large joints of meat to crème anglaise, I just always use the probe. It takes the guessing out of the picture, and you get the perfect dish every time. I think with the new love for sous-vide, and learning about controlled temperatures in food and cooking, has made it an even more useful part of the kitchen.

Daniel Newton

The Rose & Crown, Yardley Hastings

In The Kitchen

Ingredients - Serves 5-6
- 2-2.5kg Shoulder of Lamb
- 35g Fresh Rosemary
- Bulb of Garlic
- Tin of Anchovies
- 400g Washed Leeks (chopped)
- 100g Shallot (chopped)
- 150ml Double Cream
- 200ml Beef Stock
- 25g Butter
- 300g New Potatoes (optional)
- Fresh Chives

Method
1. First make the marinade by blending together the peeled garlic, anchovies and rosemary with a little olive oil. Score the shoulder of lamb and rub the mix all over. Leave to rest in fridge for at least one hour; overnight is best.
2. Place shoulder in roasting tin on a bed of roughly chopped veg (onion, carrot, celery and garlic) with a splash of water. Place it in the oven on 190ºc for 20 mins, then remove and cover the whole tin with foil. Drop the oven to 150ºc and cook for a further 4-5 hours; constantly checking and adding water if it starts to dry.
3. While the lamb is cooking, fry shallots for 3 mins and then add the leeks. Reduce the heat and cook for about 8-10 mins. Once the leeks have cooked, add in the double cream and reduce to thicken. Season and set aside.
4. Get a pan of boiling salt water, half the new potatoes and cook for 10-15 mins until cooked. Drain and leave to air dry. When ready, heat the frying pan, add the butter and melt. Then add the cooked potatoes and sauté for 5-6 mins. Season, and add the fresh chopped chives.
5. Once the lamb is cooked, you should be able to pull bone/blade out easily. Remove from tin and let it rest under the foil.
6. Place the roasting tin on the stove and deglaze with red wine and reduce. Add the beef stock and pass with a sieve. Return to the saucepan and reduce by half. Check the seasoning.
7. Serve the lamb on the creamed leeks, buttered chive potatoes and rich garlic and rosemary jus.

Slow Roasted Shoulder of Lamb, Creamed

The Vine House Hotel & Restaurant

Chef Profile

Cooking style
Traditional British with a continental modern twist. I am very precise and like to pack dishes with flavour, (my sorbet's can use a whole tray of fruit) exploring unusual marriages of tastes that really work in combination, to the mantra of only the very best will do.

Current speciality
Traditional / deconstructed / intensely flavoured / taken to the enth degree / One of my signature dishes is a favourite of regular diners and often requested – home smoked warm salmon with curry oil and garlic sauce and black pudding; oh and there is the famous 'PatPat' which has quite a following...milk marinated Goosnargh chicken liver Pate (no bitterness there!)

What do you love most about your job?
Pleasing people through the shared joy of food. It is my life and passion. I am so lucky to be doing what I enjoy and consider it my life's work.

Training or background
After training in Essex, I worked in London before moving out to the country and taking on the restoration of the Northamptonshire stone Vine House and establishing the Hotel and Restaurant more than two decades ago. Life as a Chef is a continual learning journey as I am always researching and pushing forward with my cooking, honing my skills, striving always for perfection to delight my diners.

What prompted you to become a Chef?
Being a Chef is part of my core, it was always something I wanted to do since boyhood. I've always loved food and being a chef seemed the only natural thing to do. I started in London.....met Julie, my darling wife whom diners will recognise as she works front of house whilst I am in the kitchen, and together our dream was to have our own restaurant, the rest is history.

Marcus Springett

Bubble & Squeak and Mustard Gravy

In The Kitchen

Ingredients - Serves 4

For Sausages
- 675g Steak & Kidney
- 1 Small Onion
- 1 Garlic Clove
- 1 tbsp Parsley (chopped)
- 1 Bay Leaf
- 1 tbsp Sage (chopped)
- Salt & Pepper
- 1 Egg Yolk

For Bubble & Squeak
- 115g Cooked Cabbage
- 50g Cooked Leek
- 50g Cooked Spinach
- 225g Mashed Potato
- Salt & Pepper
- Oil for pan frying

For Deep Fried Onions
- 300ml Milk
- Seasoned Flour
- Oil for deep frying
- 225g Mashed Potato
- Salt & Pepper

For Mustard Gravy
- 600ml Veal Stock
- 25g Grain Mustard
- 25g Butter (cut into pieces)
- Salt & Pepper

Method
To make the sausages: Mince all the ingredients and season. Bind together with the egg yolk. Divide the mixture into eight and roll into thick sausage shapes. Wrap each one carefully in Clingfilm and chill for about 1 hour in the fridge. Poach the wrapped sausages in simmering water for 10 minutes, then remove and dip into a bowl of cold water to refresh. Chill until required. *To prepare the onions for deep frying:* Simply slice and put into a bowl, cover with the milk and leave for about 1 hour.
1 Remove Clingfilm from the sausages and grill them on all sides for about 3 minutes until cooked. **2** Mix together the ingredients for the bubble and squeak, heat a little oil in a frying pan and fry the mixture on both sides until golden. **3** Drain the onions; dip in seasoned flour and deep fry until crispy. **4** For the gravy, bring the stock to the boil in a pan then whisk in the mustard and butter until the gravy is thick and shiny. Season to taste. *To serve:* Cut the bubble and squeak into 4 slices and place each slice in the centre of a plate. Top each slice with 2 sausages, pile the crisp onions on top, then pour a little of the mustard gravy around the outside.

behind the scenes

Chef Profile

Cooking style
Classic English, French Fusion.

Current speciality
No speciality as I would rather try all aspects of cooking. However, I follow any traditional British food with a twist.

Training or background
Two months part-time at a restaurant before two years at West Kingsway College, then 5 years of full time work.

What do you love most about your job?
The creativity I have with using different products and experimenting with seasonal produce.

What prompted you to become a Chef?
At a young age watching and helping my Mum cook.

Which seasonal produce do you look forward to?
I love looking forward to the Game season in particular.

What's your favourite food combo?
I really enjoy the softness of a pork belly with crispy crackling and a sweet sauce.

How do you like to unwind?
Cycling around the countryside.

What's your preferred home cooked meal?
A good fresh homemade burger.

The Bricklayers Arms

Martin West

In The Kitchen

Ingredients - Serves 4
- 250g Parsnips
- 100ml Balsamic Vinegar
- 100ml Double Cream
- Milk

- 15g Butter
- 12 Fresh King Scallops
- 4 Rashers of Bacon

Pre-heat oven to 160°C

Method

1 *For the Purée:* Peel the parsnips, then top and tail them. Place them into the milk and bring them to the boil. Once the parsnips are cooked thoroughly, drain the milk and put the parsnips into a food processor. Blitz them until they become a smooth texture, then add the cream and season with salt to taste.

2 *For the Bacon:* Place the bacon onto a baking tray and into a fan assisted oven for 15 minutes. Take it out and drain the water. Place it back for another five minutes, then drain any other excess water, then cut each rasher into three even sizes.

3 *For the Scallops:* Dry the scallops on a cloth and then with a small knife, take off the tough muscle on the side of the scallop. Heat up your pan to a very hot temperature, then add the butter, then the scallops. Colour the scallops on both sides to give them a nice caramelised look. Place them into the oven for two minutes and then season them just before serving, not before, as this will break the protein in the scallops.

4 *For the Balsamic Glaze:* Boil the vinegar until it reduces to a thick syrup consistency. You can flavour your glaze to your taste using any sweet condiment such as honey or plum sauce.

5 *To serve:* Making sure all the aspects are hot, put the balsamic glaze onto the plate, then using a teaspoon put three quenelles of the purée on top. Next, place the bacon slightly off centre on the purée and finally put one scallop on each quenelle of purée.

Pan Fried King Scallops with

Chez Mumtaj

Bengal Red Snapper Boatman Fish Curry

Chef Profile

Cooking style
Classical French techniques, accented with subtle Franco-Asian flavours!

Current speciality
Guinea Fowl: Pan roasted Supreme in Ras El Hanout Fricasse a la Persillade braised Savoy Cabbage, Broad Beans and Homemade Smoked Chorizo, Chicken Tikka and Wild Mushroom Pie, Truffle Game Jus.

Training or background
Trained at The Conrad Hilton Hotel School, four year degree Houston, Texas. Worked in various fine dining outlets within hotel groups Hilton, Four Seasons and Hyatt Regency.

What cookbooks would you recommend?
'Larousse Gastronomique' (the bible of French cooking), truly inspirational for menu planning/development. Also 'Seasonal Food' by Paul Waddington, a guide to what's in season, when and why.

What country do you think has the best food?
Britain of course! In all my travels around the world I would say Britain is by far the best country. Why? Answer: Multiculturalism. A rare social phenomena that we can proudly boast of.

How do you keep up with the latest cooking innovations?
For any serious chef the industry pulse is on 'The Restaurant Magazine', 'The Caterer', 'The Hotel & Caterer', 'The Stockpot' & 'Eat Out Magazine'.

What kitchen tool couldn't you live without?
The Thermomix - lightweight, versatile, multi-functional. You could even cook a curry or a stir-fry in it. Believe it or not, I'm dead serious! Grinding, chopping, pureés, steaming, braising etc. all in a jug!

What technique is simple but impressive?
Sugar corkscrews, a dessert pesentation tool that elevates a pudding to 'wow factor' status.

Chad Rahman

In The Kitchen

Ingredients

- 5 Red Snapper Fish Steaks
- 1 tbsp Kasundi Mustard Paste
- 1 tsp Black Mustard Seeds
- ½ tsp Cumin Seeds
- 4 Green Chillies
- White Pepper
- 1 tbsp Chopped Garlic
- 2 tbsp Mustard Oil
- 2 tbsp Vegetable Oil

- 1 Chopped Shallot Onion
- 1 tbsp Chopped Fresh Coriander
- 1 Sprig of Curry Leaves
- Juice of half a lemon
- Salt to taste
- 1 tsp Turmeric Powder
- ½ tsp Cumin Powder
- ½ tsp Kashmiri Chilli Powder
- 2 tbsp Yoghurt

- 2 tbsp Water
- Pinch of Saffron
- 1 tbsp Butter
- 300ml Chicken Stock
- 3 Cherry Vine Tomatoes
- 5 Baby Potatoes
- 5 Baby Aubergines

Method

Marinade for Red Snapper Steaks:
1 Wash the Red Snapper steaks thoroughly under running water making sure that all the scales are removed. Pat dry with paper towel removing any excess water. Place in mixing bowl, add salt, white pepper, ½ tsp chilli and 1tsp turmeric powder, juice of half a lemon and 1tbsp of vegetable oil. Mix all the ingredients, gently massaging the spices into the flesh of the snapper steaks, set aside for 30 mins for the marinade to permeate.
2 Heat non-stick pan with 1tbsp of vegetable oil bring to temperature,

shallow fry the snapper steaks till golden brown. Keep aside.

Poached Saffron Baby Potatoes:
Peel and wash potatoes, place in a saucepan, add chicken stock, 1tbsp salted butter, pinch of saffron, bring to boil, reduce heat to simmer until potatoes are cooked. Set aside.

Preparation of Sauce:
In a saucepan, heat 2tbsp mustard oil, add 1tsp black mustard seeds, ½ tsp cumin seeds until seeds pop and crackle. Add 3 slit green chillies, curry leaves, finely

chopped shallots and garlic. Sauté until translucent, add 1tsp turmeric, ½ tsp cumin powder, 1tbsp kasundi mustard paste and stir for 2 minutes. Add baby aubergines and cook for 5 minutes then add 2tbsp of yogurt and 2tbsp of water. Simmer for 10 mins, place fried snapper steaks into saucepan and simmer for further 3 mins. Add 3 cherry vine tomatoes until sauce thickens, add salt to taste. Finally, add freshly chopped coriander to sauce and take off heat. Serve with steamed rice.

Happy Cooking
Bon Appetit !!!!!

Chef Profile

Cooking style
Classical British with French twist.

What dish are you most proud of?
Millefeuille of Duck Medallion with Apple and Figs.

What is your favourite British food?
Quality local British Beef, hung for 21/28 days and cooked any way.

How do you source your ingredients?
Most of our ingredients are sourced local where possible. This ensures the freshest of produce which is the key to consistent quality dishes.

What would you say has been the highlight of your chef career?
Serving the Queen at the Houses of Parliament and achieving an "AA Rosette Award for Culinary Excellence" for the Nags Head within only 6 months of opening.

What advice would you give any up and coming chefs?
Preparation is the key prior to the service which can make or break a lunch or dinner session. You obviously cook according to the fixed menu but be adventurous with your menu specials of the day and look to the daily markets for unusual fresh fish and meats of the day. By mixing your menu, this stimulates your interest in being passionate about food.

Do you have any cooking tips you can share with us?
Never forget to correctly season your dishes.

Have you set yourself any goals for the future?
Continue and win further accolades and to earn a Michelin star.

Alan Bell

The Nags Head, Great Missenden

In The Kitchen

Ingredients - Serves 4
- 1 Leek
- 4 Duck Breasts
- 2 Bramley Apples
- 4 Figs
- 12 Rice Sheets
- 1 ltr Cider Vinegar
- 100g Honey
- 1¼ pint Brown Duck Stock
- Sea Salt & White Pepper
- 1 Clove Garlic
- 1 Pumpkin 1.5kg
- 4 ltr Cream
- 50g Grated Gruyere
- Grilled Pumpkin and Sesame Seeds

Method
1. Brush the top of the rice sheets with clarified butter and sprinkle a mixture of grilled pumpkin and sesame seeds. Cook the rice sheets in the oven for 1 minute at 200ºC.
2. Pan fry the duck breast to seal. Wrap the leek around the duck breast and cook for 7 minutes at 200ºC. Cut duck breast into 3 medallions when cooked to present.
3. *To make the Compote:* Cook the bramley apples and figs in the oven for 3 minutes. Layer the cooked rice sheets between the apple and fig compote to produce the millefeuille.
4. *To make the Cider and Honey Jus:* Reduce the cider vinegar with honey until golden caramel colour and add duck stock. Reduce and season to taste.
5. *To make the Pumpkin Gratin:* Slice the peeled pumpkin and cook at 180ºC with 1 clove of garlic and add 4 x ltrs cream and seasoning. When cooked add the gruyere and place the dish under the grill to gratin. Use a blow torch for even crispness. Enjoy!

Millefeuille of Duck Medallion with Apple and

ORDER THE FOODIE GUIDE FOR A FRIEND

'The Perfect Gift'

Step 1 Fill in the name and address details of the recipient.

Step 2 Write your personal message (this cut out section will be enclosed with the guide).

Step 3 Fill in your name and address details on reverse of message section.

Step 4 Return completed form to us with a cheque for £6 per book (p&p FREE).

N.B. Guides are despatched via Royal Mail. We will send you a receipt once despatched.

Please make cheques payable to The Square Design & Print Co Ltd and post (no need for a stamp) to:-
Freepost RSKB-RHRA-RZBT, The Foodie Guide, 373 Welford Road, Northampton NN2 8PT.

Step 1

Fill in the name and address details of the recipient.

Please post to:

Name

Address

Postcode

Write your message below and then **fill in your details on the reverse -**
we will do the rest...

Step 2

Write your personal message (this section will be enclosed with the guide).

Your message:

THE FOODIE GUIDE

Your favourite restaurants, delis and farm shops

'The Perfect Gift'

vouchers 2014

THE FOODIE GUIDE has been sent to you from:

Name

Address

Postcode

Tel

Email

▶ **Step 3**
Fill in **your** name and address details.

▶ **Step 4**
Return form with your cheque to:
Freepost RSKB-RHRA-RZBT,
The Foodie Guide,
373 Welford Road,
Northampton, NN2 8PT.

lifestyle

lifestyle

lifestyle

lifestyle

OLIVER
GARDEN

Eden

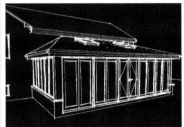

Kew

OliverJamesGardenRooms.co.uk   01908 367177

JAMES

ROOMS

Rousham

Wisley

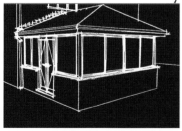

info@OliverJamesGardenRooms.co.uk

lifestyle

The Day Spa
Whittlebury Hall

Day Spa, Hotel & Spa
Breaks from just £59pp*

Simple
indulgence...

Escape with our simply indulgent offers

Enjoy a rejuvenating escape with friends and family in our **award-winning facilities** and take time out to refresh in the luxurious **Whittlebury Hall Hotel and Spa**. (approx 15 mins drive from Milton Keynes).

Book online today at **www.whittleburyhall.co.uk**
or call us on **0845 400 0002** and quote FOODIE

*Terms & Conditions apply. Subject to availability. See website for full details. pp=per person.

WOBURN
The Inn at Woburn

PRIVATE DINING AND
SPECIAL OCCASIONS

Set in the heart of the Georgian village of Woburn, the hotel is owned and managed by the historic Woburn Abbey estate. 2013 has seen a stylish refurbishment of the hotel to reflect the best of modern comforts for an understated, yet classic look and feel.

The hotel's restaurant, Olivier's, continues to flourish under the auspices of Executive Chef Olivier Bertho and is proud to have achieved The Foodie Guide Bedfordshire Restaurant for 2010, 2011 and 2012.

The hotel offers a perfect setting for hosting private dining and special occasions including anniversary, birthday and family celebrations. The Red Room or Canaletto Suite are available for guests to host private celebrations and can accommodate small intimate groups from just 8 to larger gatherings of up to 80 guests.

For the perfect ending to the celebrations, the hotel offers 48 bedrooms and 7 delightfully designed individual cottages for guests.

For further information, or to discuss hosting your special occasion at The Inn at Woburn, please contact Karen Torrington on **01525 290441**

The Inn at Woburn, George Street, Woburn, Bedfordshire, MK17 9PX
Tel: (01525) 290441 • **Fax:** (01525) 290432 • **Email:** inn@woburn.co.uk

woburn.co.uk

lifestyle

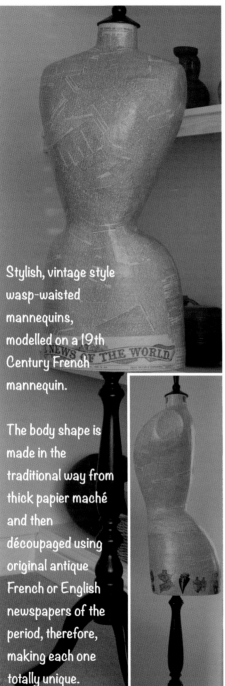

Stylish, vintage style wasp-waisted mannequins, modelled on a 19th Century French mannequin.

The body shape is made in the traditional way from thick papier maché and then découpaged using original antique French or English newspapers of the period, therefore, making each one totally unique.

ourglass
mannequins

Beautiful corset style laced-back mannequins using quality drape fabrics such as Laura Ashley. Can be made to order in your choice of fabric.

The main body is a high density polystyrene and the stand is made from beech timber and comes in three different colours; natural beech, white or black.

For more information please email:
info@hourglassmannequins.co.uk

SPECIAL FOODIE

Voucher

FREE BOTTLE OF WINE

When 2 adults dine Monday - Sunday evening
from the à la carte menu only
at Olivier's Restaurant

Valid until 30th September 2014

Terms & Conditions on reverse.

OLIVIER'S RESTAURANT

George St, Woburn, Bedfordshire MK17 9PX
Tel: 01525 290441 **Fax:** 01525 290432
Email: inn@woburn.co.uk
www.woburn.co.uk/inn

SPECIAL FOODIE

Voucher

10% OFF

AT DELICATESSEN ESTRELLA
WHEN SPENDING £20 OR MORE

Valid until 30th September 2014

Terms & Conditions on reverse.

DELICATESSEN ESTRELLA

2A High Street, Winslow, Buckinghamshire MK18 3HF
Tel: 01296 712466 **www.delicatessenestrella.co.uk**

SPECIAL FOODIE

Voucher

25% OFF

TOTAL FOOD BILL AT RAJDHANI
(exclusions apply please see reverse)

Valid until 30th September 2014

Terms & Conditions on reverse.

Rajdhani

Central Milton Keynes MK9 3NT
Tel: 01908 392299
Fax: 01908 392541
www.rajdhanimk.com

Terms and Conditions

- The Special Foodie Vouchers in Edition 11 of THE FOODIE GUIDE are valid until 30th September 2014.
- This voucher entitles the bearer to a free bottle of house selected red or white wine when 2 adults dine from the evening à la carte menu only, Monday to Sunday. Offer available for over 21's only.
- Please bring this completed voucher to redeem this offer.
- Only one voucher may be redeemed against the final bill inclusive of VAT.
- The condition of the voucher on presentation and its acceptance is at the discretion of Olivier's Restaurant at The Inn at Woburn.
- Exchange or sale of this voucher is strictly prohibited.
- Voucher limited to single use and photocopies will not be accepted.
- This voucher may not be used in conjunction with any other offers.

IT MAY BE HELPFUL IF YOU MENTION THE USE OF THIS VOUCHER *WHEN ORDERING* YOUR MEAL

Name

Address

Postcode   Email

If you would not like your details passed on to any third parties please tick this box ❐

Terms and Conditions

- The Special Foodie Vouchers in Edition 11 of THE FOODIE GUIDE are valid until 30th September 2014.
- This voucher entitles the bearer to 10% discount when spending £20 or more at Delicatessen Estrella, Winslow.
- Please bring this completed voucher to redeem this offer.
- Only one voucher may be redeemed per transaction.
- The condition of the voucher on presentation and its acceptance is at the discretion of Delicatessen Estrella, Winslow.
- Exchange or sale of this voucher is strictly prohibited.
- Voucher limited to single use and photocopies will not be accepted.
- This voucher does not have any cash value and may not be used in conjunction with any other offers.

Name

Address

Postcode   Email

If you would not like your details passed on to any third parties please tick this box ❐

Terms and Conditions

- The Special Foodie Vouchers in Edition 11 of THE FOODIE GUIDE are valid until 30th September 2014.
- This voucher entitles the bearer to 25% off the total food bill when dining in the restaurant; excluding Buffets, all Set Meals, Thali's, Desserts and Beverages, at Rajdhani, Central Milton Keynes.
- The maximum saving is £25.
- Please bring this completed voucher to redeem this offer.
- Only one voucher may be redeemed against the final bill.
- The condition of the voucher on presentation and its acceptance is at the discretion of Rajdhani, Central Milton Keynes.
- Exchange or sale of this voucher is strictly prohibited.
- Voucher limited to single use and photocopies will not be accepted.
- This voucher may not be used in conjunction with any other offers.

IT MAY BE HELPFUL IF YOU MENTION THE USE OF THIS VOUCHER *WHEN ORDERING* YOUR MEAL

Name

Address

Postcode   Email

If you would not like your details passed on to any third parties please tick this box ❐

SPECIAL FOODIE
Voucher
HALF PRICE
BOTTLE OF WINE
AT THE RED LION HOTEL, SALFORD
when you buy a minimum of one main course
Valid until 30th September 2014
Terms & Conditions on reverse.

Salford, Milton Keynes MK17 8AZ
Tel: 01908 583117
Email: info@redlionhotel.eu
www.redlionhotel.eu

RedLion
COUNTRY HOTEL

SPECIAL FOODIE
Voucher
10% OFF
AT MURRAYS AT WHITTLEBURY HALL
SUBJECT TO AVAILABILITY. OFFER EXCLUDES SATURDAYS.
Valid until 30th September 2014
Terms & Conditions on reverse.

Northants NN12 8QH
Tel: 0845 400 0001
www.whittleburyhall.co.uk/murrays

SPECIAL FOODIE
Voucher
BUY 3 MAIN COURSES AND
GET THE 4TH FREE
(STEAK COUNTER NOT INCLUDED)
AT THE CARRINGTON ARMS
Valid until 30th September 2014

THE CARRINGTON ARMS

Moulsoe, Newport Pagnell MK16 0HB
Tel: 01908 218050 www.thecarringtonarms.co.uk

Terms and Conditions

- The Special Foodie Vouchers in Edition 11 of THE FOODIE GUIDE are valid until 30th September 2014.
- This voucher entitles the bearer to a half price bottle of wine when buying a minimum of one main course meal at The Red Lion Hotel, Salford.
- Please bring this completed voucher to redeem this offer.
- Only one voucher may be redeemed against the final bill inclusive of VAT.
- The condition of the voucher on presentation and its acceptance is at the discretion of The Red Lion Hotel, Salford.
- No photocopy or any other reproduction of the voucher will be accepted.
- This voucher does not have any cash value and may not be used in conjunction with any other offers.

IT MAY BE HELPFUL IF YOU MENTION THE USE OF THIS VOUCHER *WHEN ORDERING* YOUR MEAL

Name
Address
Postcode   Email
If you would not like your details passed on to any third parties please tick this box ❐

Terms and Conditions

- The Special Foodie Vouchers in Edition 11 of THE FOODIE GUIDE are valid until 30th September 2014.
- This voucher entitles the bearer to 10% off at Murrays at Whittlebury Hall, excludes Saturdays and subject to availability.
- Please bring this completed voucher to redeem this offer.
- Only one voucher may be redeemed against the final bill inclusive of VAT.
- The condition of the voucher on presentation and its acceptance is at the discretion of Murrays at Whittlebury Hall.
- Exchange or sale of this voucher is strictly prohibited.
- Voucher limited to single use and photocopies will not be accepted.
- This voucher may not be used in conjunction with any other offers.

IT MAY BE HELPFUL IF YOU MENTION THE USE OF THIS VOUCHER *WHEN ORDERING* YOUR MEAL

Name
Address
Postcode   Email
If you would not like your details passed on to any third parties please tick this box ❐

Terms and Conditions

- The Special Foodie Vouchers in Edition 11 of THE FOODIE GUIDE are valid until 30th September 2014.
- This voucher entitles the bearer to a free 4th main course when 3 main courses are purchased (Steak Counter not included) at The Carrington Arms, Moulsoe.
- Only one voucher may be redeemed against the final bill.
- Please bring this completed voucher to redeem this offer.
- The condition of the voucher on presentation and its acceptance is at the discretion of The Carrington Arms.
- Exchange or sale of this voucher is strictly prohibited.
- Voucher limited to single use and photocopies will not be accepted.
- This voucher may not be used in conjunction with any other offers.

IT MAY BE HELPFUL IF YOU MENTION THE USE OF THIS VOUCHER *WHEN ORDERING* YOUR MEAL

Name
Address
Postcode   Email
If you would not like your details passed on to any third parties please tick this box ❐

The Foodie Voucher

This voucher entitles the bearer on presentation to 10% discount off final bill inclusive of VAT

Valid only at participating establishments displaying a GOLD 10% symbol
Valid until 30th September 2014
See terms and conditions overleaf

© The Foodie Voucher. This voucher entitles the bearer on presentation to 10% discount. Valid only at participating establishments displaying a GOLD 10% symbol on their advertisement in The Foodie Guide.

The Foodie Voucher

This voucher entitles the bearer on presentation to 10% discount off final bill inclusive of VAT

Valid only at participating establishments displaying a GOLD 10% symbol
Valid until 30th September 2014
See terms and conditions overleaf

© The Foodie Voucher. This voucher entitles the bearer on presentation to 10% discount. Valid only at participating establishments displaying a GOLD 10% symbol on their advertisement in The Foodie Guide.

The Foodie Voucher

This voucher entitles the bearer on presentation to 10% discount off final bill inclusive of VAT

Valid only at participating establishments displaying a GOLD 10% symbol
Valid until 30th September 2014
See terms and conditions overleaf

© The Foodie Voucher. This voucher entitles the bearer on presentation to 10% discount. Valid only at participating establishments displaying a GOLD 10% symbol on their advertisement in The Foodie Guide.

Terms and Conditions

- The vouchers presented in this edition of The Foodie Guide are valid until 30th September 2014.
- Only one voucher may be redeemed against the final bill inclusive of VAT.
- The final bill inclusive of VAT must be to the value of £30.00 or more to qualify.
- The voucher is valid only in participating establishments which display the relevant voucher symbol on their display advert **(please take note of any additional conditions thereon)** and with the participating establishment bearing the cost of the offer.
- The condition of the voucher on presentation and its acceptance is at the discretion of the participating establishment.
- No photocopy or any other reproduction of the voucher will be accepted.
- These vouchers do not have any cash value and may not be used in conjunction with any other offers.

IT MAY BE HELPFUL IF YOU MENTION THE USE OF THIS VOUCHER **WHEN ORDERING** YOUR MEAL

If you would like to be kept informed of any promotional offers from the establishment, please fill in your name and address below
Name
Address
Postcode   Email
If you would not like your details passed on to any third parties please tick this box ❒

Terms and Conditions

- The vouchers presented in this edition of The Foodie Guide are valid until 30th September 2014.
- Only one voucher may be redeemed against the final bill inclusive of VAT.
- The final bill inclusive of VAT must be to the value of £30.00 or more to qualify.
- The voucher is valid only in participating establishments which display the relevant voucher symbol on their display advert **(please take note of any additional conditions thereon)** and with the participating establishment bearing the cost of the offer.
- The condition of the voucher on presentation and its acceptance is at the discretion of the participating establishment.
- No photocopy or any other reproduction of the voucher will be accepted.
- These vouchers do not have any cash value and may not be used in conjunction with any other offers.

IT MAY BE HELPFUL IF YOU MENTION THE USE OF THIS VOUCHER **WHEN ORDERING** YOUR MEAL

If you would like to be kept informed of any promotional offers from the establishment, please fill in your name and address below
Name
Address
Postcode   Email
If you would not like your details passed on to any third parties please tick this box ❒

Terms and Conditions

- The vouchers presented in this edition of The Foodie Guide are valid until 30th September 2014.
- Only one voucher may be redeemed against the final bill inclusive of VAT.
- The final bill inclusive of VAT must be to the value of £30.00 or more to qualify.
- The voucher is valid only in participating establishments which display the relevant voucher symbol on their display advert **(please take note of any additional conditions thereon)** and with the participating establishment bearing the cost of the offer.
- The condition of the voucher on presentation and its acceptance is at the discretion of the participating establishment.
- No photocopy or any other reproduction of the voucher will be accepted.
- These vouchers do not have any cash value and may not be used in conjunction with any other offers.

IT MAY BE HELPFUL IF YOU MENTION THE USE OF THIS VOUCHER **WHEN ORDERING** YOUR MEAL

If you would like to be kept informed of any promotional offers from the establishment, please fill in your name and address below
Name
Address
Postcode   Email
If you would not like your details passed on to any third parties please tick this box ❒

The Foodie Voucher

This voucher entitles the bearer on presentation to £5 discount off final bill inclusive of VAT

Valid only at participating establishments displaying a GREEN £5 symbol
Valid until 30th September 2014

See terms and conditions overleaf

© The Foodie Voucher.
This voucher entitles the bearer on presentation to £5 discount. Valid only at participating establishments displaying a GREEN £5 symbol on their advertisement in The Foodie Guide.

The Foodie Voucher

This voucher entitles the bearer on presentation to £5 discount off final bill inclusive of VAT

Valid only at participating establishments displaying a GREEN £5 symbol
Valid until 30th September 2014

See terms and conditions overleaf

© The Foodie Voucher.
This voucher entitles the bearer on presentation to £5 discount. Valid only at participating establishments displaying a GREEN £5 symbol on their advertisement in The Foodie Guide.

The Foodie Voucher

This voucher entitles the bearer on presentation to £5 discount off final bill inclusive of VAT

Valid only at participating establishments displaying a GREEN £5 symbol
Valid until 30th September 2014

See terms and conditions overleaf

© The Foodie Voucher.
This voucher entitles the bearer on presentation to £5 discount. Valid only at participating establishments displaying a GREEN £5 symbol on their advertisement in The Foodie Guide.

Terms and Conditions

- The vouchers presented in this edition of The Foodie Guide are valid until 30th September 2014.
- Only one voucher may be redeemed against the final bill inclusive of VAT.
- The final bill inclusive of VAT must be to the value of £30.00 or more to qualify.
- The voucher is valid only in participating establishments which display the relevant voucher symbol on their display advert **(please take note of any additional conditions thereon)** and with the participating establishment bearing the cost of the offer.
- The condition of the voucher on presentation and its acceptance is at the discretion of the participating establishment.
- No photocopy or any other reproduction of the voucher will be accepted.
- These vouchers do not have any cash value and may not be used in conjunction with any other offers.

IT MAY BE HELPFUL IF YOU MENTION THE USE OF THIS VOUCHER **WHEN ORDERING** YOUR MEAL

If you would like to be kept informed of any promotional offers from the establishment, please fill in your name and address below
Name
Address
Postcode   Email
If you would not like your details passed on to any third parties please tick this box ❐

Terms and Conditions

- The vouchers presented in this edition of The Foodie Guide are valid until 30th September 2014.
- Only one voucher may be redeemed against the final bill inclusive of VAT.
- The final bill inclusive of VAT must be to the value of £30.00 or more to qualify.
- The voucher is valid only in participating establishments which display the relevant voucher symbol on their display advert **(please take note of any additional conditions thereon)** and with the participating establishment bearing the cost of the offer.
- The condition of the voucher on presentation and its acceptance is at the discretion of the participating establishment.
- No photocopy or any other reproduction of the voucher will be accepted.
- These vouchers do not have any cash value and may not be used in conjunction with any other offers.

IT MAY BE HELPFUL IF YOU MENTION THE USE OF THIS VOUCHER **WHEN ORDERING** YOUR MEAL

If you would like to be kept informed of any promotional offers from the establishment, please fill in your name and address below
Name
Address
Postcode   Email
If you would not like your details passed on to any third parties please tick this box ❐

Terms and Conditions

- The vouchers presented in this edition of The Foodie Guide are valid until 30th September 2014.
- Only one voucher may be redeemed against the final bill inclusive of VAT.
- The final bill inclusive of VAT must be to the value of £30.00 or more to qualify.
- The voucher is valid only in participating establishments which display the relevant voucher symbol on their display advert **(please take note of any additional conditions thereon)** and with the participating establishment bearing the cost of the offer.
- The condition of the voucher on presentation and its acceptance is at the discretion of the participating establishment.
- No photocopy or any other reproduction of the voucher will be accepted.
- These vouchers do not have any cash value and may not be used in conjunction with any other offers.

IT MAY BE HELPFUL IF YOU MENTION THE USE OF THIS VOUCHER **WHEN ORDERING** YOUR MEAL

If you would like to be kept informed of any promotional offers from the establishment, please fill in your name and address below
Name
Address
Postcode   Email
If you would not like your details passed on to any third parties please tick this box ❐

The Foodie Voucher

This voucher entitles the bearer on presentation to one bottle of house wine

Valid only at participating establishments displaying a SILVER BOTTLE symbol
Valid until 30th September 2014
See terms and conditions overleaf

© The Foodie Voucher. This voucher entitles the bearer on presentation to one bottle of house wine. Valid only at participating establishments displaying a SILVER BOTTLE symbol on their advertisement in The Foodie Guide.

The Foodie Voucher

This voucher entitles the bearer on presentation to one bottle of house wine

Valid only at participating establishments displaying a SILVER BOTTLE symbol
Valid until 30th September 2014
See terms and conditions overleaf

© The Foodie Voucher. This voucher entitles the bearer on presentation to one bottle of house wine. Valid only at participating establishments displaying a SILVER BOTTLE symbol on their advertisement in The Foodie Guide.

The Foodie Voucher

This voucher entitles the bearer on presentation to one bottle of house wine

Valid only at participating establishments displaying a SILVER BOTTLE symbol
Valid until 30th September 2014
See terms and conditions overleaf

© The Foodie Voucher. This voucher entitles the bearer on presentation to one bottle of house wine. Valid only at participating establishments displaying a SILVER BOTTLE symbol on their advertisement in The Foodie Guide.

Terms and Conditions

- The vouchers presented in this edition of The Foodie Guide are valid until 30th September 2014.
- Only one voucher may be redeemed against the final bill inclusive of VAT.
- The final bill inclusive of VAT must be to the value of £30.00 or more to qualify.
- The voucher is valid only in participating establishments which display the relevant voucher symbol on their display advert **(please take note of any additional conditions thereon)** and with the participating establishment bearing the cost of the offer.
- The condition of the voucher on presentation and its acceptance is at the discretion of the participating establishment.
- No photocopy or any other reproduction of the voucher will be accepted.
- These vouchers do not have any cash value and may not be used in conjunction with any other offers.

IT MAY BE HELPFUL IF YOU MENTION THE USE OF THIS VOUCHER **WHEN ORDERING** YOUR MEAL

If you would like to be kept informed of any promotional offers from the establishment, please fill in your name and address below
Name
Address
Postcode   Email
If you would not like your details passed on to any third parties please tick this box ❒

Terms and Conditions

- The vouchers presented in this edition of The Foodie Guide are valid until 30th September 2014.
- Only one voucher may be redeemed against the final bill inclusive of VAT.
- The final bill inclusive of VAT must be to the value of £30.00 or more to qualify.
- The voucher is valid only in participating establishments which display the relevant voucher symbol on their display advert **(please take note of any additional conditions thereon)** and with the participating establishment bearing the cost of the offer.
- The condition of the voucher on presentation and its acceptance is at the discretion of the participating establishment.
- No photocopy or any other reproduction of the voucher will be accepted.
- These vouchers do not have any cash value and may not be used in conjunction with any other offers.

IT MAY BE HELPFUL IF YOU MENTION THE USE OF THIS VOUCHER **WHEN ORDERING** YOUR MEAL

If you would like to be kept informed of any promotional offers from the establishment, please fill in your name and address below
Name
Address
Postcode   Email
If you would not like your details passed on to any third parties please tick this box ❒

Terms and Conditions

- The vouchers presented in this edition of The Foodie Guide are valid until 30th September 2014.
- Only one voucher may be redeemed against the final bill inclusive of VAT.
- The final bill inclusive of VAT must be to the value of £30.00 or more to qualify.
- The voucher is valid only in participating establishments which display the relevant voucher symbol on their display advert **(please take note of any additional conditions thereon)** and with the participating establishment bearing the cost of the offer.
- The condition of the voucher on presentation and its acceptance is at the discretion of the participating establishment.
- No photocopy or any other reproduction of the voucher will be accepted.
- These vouchers do not have any cash value and may not be used in conjunction with any other offers.

IT MAY BE HELPFUL IF YOU MENTION THE USE OF THIS VOUCHER **WHEN ORDERING** YOUR MEAL

If you would like to be kept informed of any promotional offers from the establishment, please fill in your name and address below
Name
Address
Postcode   Email
If you would not like your details passed on to any third parties please tick this box ❒

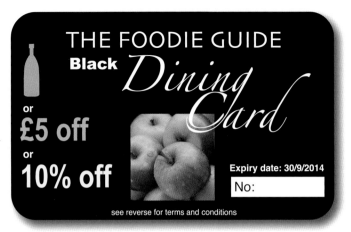

THE FOODIE GUIDE

Black *Dining Card*

or
£5 off
or
10% off

Expiry date: 30/9/2014

No:

see reverse for terms and conditions

Order your exclusive

Black *Dining Card*

**LIMITED EDITION
only available to
THE FOODIE GUIDE
readers**

Use your Black Dining Card as often as you like and **you** choose which offer you would prefer -
either a free Bottle of House Wine, £5 off *or* 10% off.

To apply for your Black Dining Card please fill in the form below and send (no stamp required) together with a cheque for £10 to:
FREEPOST RSKB-RHRA-RZBT, The Foodie Guide, 373 Welford Rd, Northampton, NN2 8PT.
Alternatively, order online at **www.thefoodieguide.co.uk**

Cardholder Name . . . .

Address . . . .

. . . .

. . . .

Postcode . . . .

Email . . . .

Tel. . . . .

To receive your exclusive Black Dining Card please enclose a cheque for £10
payable to The Square Design & Print Co Ltd. Only one card per cardholder will be
issued. Every card has a unique number and can only be issued once.
No replacements will be supplied. PLEASE READ THE RULES OF USE.

CARDHOLDER RULES OF USE
1. THE FOODIE GUIDE Black Dining Card may not be used in
   conjunction with any other offers, including FOODIE Vouchers.
2. The card entitles the cardholder to choose **either** £5 off, 10% off **or** a
   Bottle of House Wine when spending £30 or more on any day of the
   week and at any time, except on the following: **NOT ACCEPTED
   during December, Mothers Day, Fathers Day or Valentines Day.**
3. Only one card up to a maximum of 6 covers per table/party may be
   used with a minimum total spend of £30.
4. The card is only accepted at participating
   restaurants displaying The Black Dining Card **DC**
   symbol within THE FOODIE GUIDE Edition 11.
5. This card has no cash value and is valid until 30/09/2014.
6. Cardholders must mention THE FOODIE GUIDE Black Dining Card
   when making a telephone booking. Failure to do so may result in the
   offer being refused.

the black dining card

Join the growing FOODIE family and visit our website

Become a "Taste Buddy" and recommend / review restaurants.
Visit the shop to order FOODIE vouchers, a black dining card or a book.
Watch video clips of local chefs at work or check out the latest news from your favourite restaurants, delis and farm shops.

www.thefoodieguide.co.uk

THE FOODIE AWARD
2014

photograph courtesy of Murrays Restaurant, Whittlebury Hall

NOMINATE
YOUR FAVOURITE RESTAURANT
AND YOU COULD
WIN A MEAL FOR TWO!

We would like to hear from you, so nominate your favourite restaurant in Beds, Bucks, Herts or Northants for THE FOODIE Award. Just fill in the details below and send the form back to us. All forms returned to us by the closing date will be entered into a draw, the lucky winner of which will receive a meal for two at one of our four award winning restaurants.

Please only nominate ONE establishment and take into consideration the quality of food, the service, the price and the surroundings before making your choice.

I would like to nominate: _____ **for THE FOODIE Award**

because _____

_____

Closing date for all nominations is 31st July 2014. (Winners of the current award will be published in the next edition of THE FOODIE GUIDE).

To be entered into the free draw please fill in your details below and then post back (NO STAMP REQUIRED) to:
Freepost RSKB-RHRA-RZBT, The Foodie Guide, 373 Welford Road, Northampton NN2 8PT.

Name: _____

Address: _____

_____ **Postcode:** _____

Telephone: _____ **Email:** _____

*Terms and conditions apply. The meal for two is excluding drinks.

We only include restaurants in THE FOODIE GUIDE which have been recommended by *you*, so please keep sending in your comments and together we shall maintain the high standard you expect.

You can send your comments via email to: paul@thefoodieguide.co.uk
or post to: Freepost RSKB-RHRA-RZBT, The Foodie Guide, 373 Welford Road, Northampton NN2 8PT.

SECRET DINERS ONLY

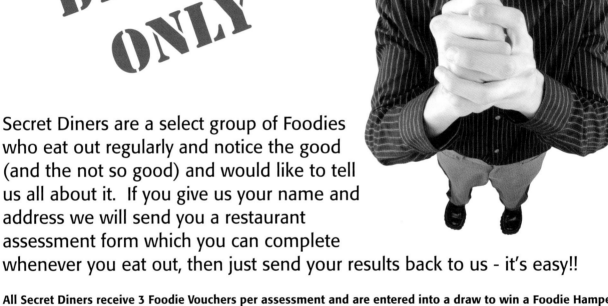

Secret Diners are a select group of Foodies who eat out regularly and notice the good (and the not so good) and would like to tell us all about it. If you give us your name and address we will send you a restaurant assessment form which you can complete whenever you eat out, then just send your results back to us - it's easy!!

All Secret Diners receive 3 Foodie Vouchers per assessment and are entered into a draw to win a Foodie Hamper. Closing date for the draw is 30th June 2014.

WOULD YOU LIKE TO BE A SECRET DINER? **YES** ☐   **NO** ☐

ARE YOUR NAME AND ADDRESS DETAILS OVERLEAF? **YES** ☐   **NO** ☐   (if NO please enter your details below)

Name: _____

Address: _____

_____ Postcode: _____

Telephone: _____ Email: _____

extra vouchers ! FREE !

The Foodie Voucher
This voucher entitles the bearer on presentation to 10% discount off final bill inclusive of VAT

Valid only at participating establishments displaying a GOLD 10% symbol
Valid until 30th September 2014
See terms and conditions overleaf

Now that you are a FOODIE GUIDE owner, we know you are serious about your food, so register your details with us and we will send you **2 extra FOODIE vouchers ABSOLUTELY FREE - or 4 vouchers if you fill in our survey on the reverse too**.

Please fill in your details below, tear this page out and send back (NO STAMP REQUIRED) to the following address:-
FREEPOST RSKB-RHRA-RZBT, The Foodie Guide, 373 Welford Road, Northampton NN2 8PT.

First Name: .... **Surname**: ....

Address:..

....

.... **Postcode**: ....

Email: ....

Tel: ....

If you would like to order extra copies of THE FOODIE GUIDE at **£6** each (**Postage & Packing FREE!!!!**) please send a cheque payable to The Square Design & Print Co Ltd and indicate how many copies you would like. Thank you.

Please send me [ ] copies. I enclose a cheque for [£]

THE FOODIE GUIDE Consumer Survey

1. Title: Mr / Mrs / Miss / Ms / Other (please state)

2. Name: . . . .

3. House No: . . . .

4. Postcode: . . . .

5. Email: . . . .

6. Age: Under 25 ❐   26-35 ❐   36-50 ❐   50+ ❐

7. What do you find most interesting/useful about The Foodie Guide (tick all that apply)

    Restaurants ❐   Chef Profiles ❐   Recipes ❐   Fine Foods & Wines ❐   Lifestyle ❐   Vouchers ❐

8. Do you use the vouchers? Yes ❐   No ❐   (if no, go to question 11)

9. Which vouchers do you use most often? £5 ❐   10% ❐   Bottle of wine ❐   Special ❐

10. How often do you use the vouchers

    weekly ❐   fortnightly ❐   monthly ❐   quarterly ❐   yearly ❐

11. If you don't use the vouchers is this because of the following (tick all that apply)

    Embarrassment ❐   Forgetting ❐   Not valuable enough ❐

    Restaurant doesn't accept vouchers ❐   Other (please state) ❐ . . . .

12. How often do you refer to The Foodie Guide

    weekly ❐   fortnightly ❐   monthly ❐   quarterly ❐   yearly ❐

13. Would you buy The Foodie Guide as a gift for somebody? Yes ❐   No ❐

14. What's the best feature of The Foodie Guide?

15. What's the worst feature of The Foodie Guide? . . . .

16. How would you improve The Foodie Guide? . . . .

17. Which vouchers would you like for filling in this survey?

    £5 ❐   10% ❐   Bottle of wine ❐

18. Any other feedback . . . .

    . . . .